Everything You Know About London Is Wrong

For Holly Grace Brown

First published in the United Kingdom in 2016 by
Batsford
43 Great Ormond Street
London
WC1N 3HZ
An imprint of Pavilion Books Company Ltd

ISBN: 9781849943604

A CIP catalogue record for this book is available from the British
Library.

20 19 18
10 9 8 7 6 5 4 3 2

Reproduction by Mission Productions, Hong Kong
Printed by 1010 Printing International Limited, China

This book can be ordered direct from the publisher
at the website www.pavilionbooks.com, or try your
local bookshop.

Everything You Know About London Is Wrong

Matt Brown

BATSFORD

Contents

Introduction

The streets of London are paved with gold. I learnt this as a child. It is a lie.

Later, I cowered from Sweeney Todd and cheered for Dick Whittington's cat in pantomime. They never existed.

I was fed stories of far-off London. I lapped up tales of a fog-haunted city, where gents in bowler hats flowed over London Bridge. In the East End, chirpy cockneys rubbed shoulders with cheeky pickpockets, pearly kings and tap-dancing chimney sweeps. I was deceived.

I came to live in London. Further assumptions were proved wrong. You are nearly always more than six feet away from a rat. The M25 motorway does not mark the boundary of London. The river is not filthy (not usually). It does, sometimes, stop raining.

You live in London long enough and you're sure to accumulate a head full of trivia about the city. Savoy Court, for example, which leads off the Strand to the Savoy Hotel, is the only place in the UK where you must drive on the right. Trafalgar Square contains the world's smallest police station. Coco Chanel's initials can be found on every Westminster lamp post. Guess what? Wrong. Wrong. Wrong. I began to suspect that, to a close approximation, *everything* I knew about London was wrong.

This book began life as a short article on the Londonist website in 2011. I briefly sketched out the truth behind a half-dozen city myths, including the one about the gullible American who thought he'd bought Tower Bridge, and the tenacious falsehood that the landmark we all know as 'Big Ben' was ever officially called St Stephen's Tower. The piece hit a nerve. Over 70 people commented, adding extra detail or presenting their own myth-busting research. Londoners love to nitpick.

And so the idea has developed into a book. In these pages, you will find dozens of assertions about the capital – from the major misconceptions of first-time visitors, to the more quirky anecdotes that are the stock-in-trade of tour guides.

Each section starts with a commonly peddled 'fact', followed by a sound debunking. I'm very aware that the four most tiresome words in the English language are: 'I think you'll find ...'. To that end, I've tried to avoid a supercilious tone in favour of something more light-hearted. My aim is to help readers think a little deeper about this great city, and to have a lot of fun in the process.

I have not covered the supernatural. London is one big rattling closet of ghost stories, from spectral hounds to phantom squirrels. To my mind, all are patently untrue, but there remains no way to prove a non-existence. Likewise, I've left well alone the folk tales and origin stories of London. The city was probably not founded by a King Lud, nor the Trojan hero Brutus. Nor was London ever guarded by the giants Gog and Magog. The Trafalgar Square lions will not spring to life when Big Ben strikes 13, nor has the eponymous statue of Queen Anne's Gate ever been seen to roam that thoroughfare. London, however, must be left with some of its magic. For those stories, and other folkloric traditions, I would direct you to the wonderful *London Lore* (2010) by Steve Roud. The one exception I've made in this area is the dubious legend that the kingdom will fall when the ravens flee the Tower of London. You will see why.

This book seeks to point out common errors about London. That means I'm likely to acquire a certain amount of egg on my face if someone spots the inevitable mistakes in my own writing or research. I welcome any correction, qualification, addition, contradiction, refutation or other form of feedback. Just don't use the words 'I think you'll find ...'

Let the nitpicking begin!

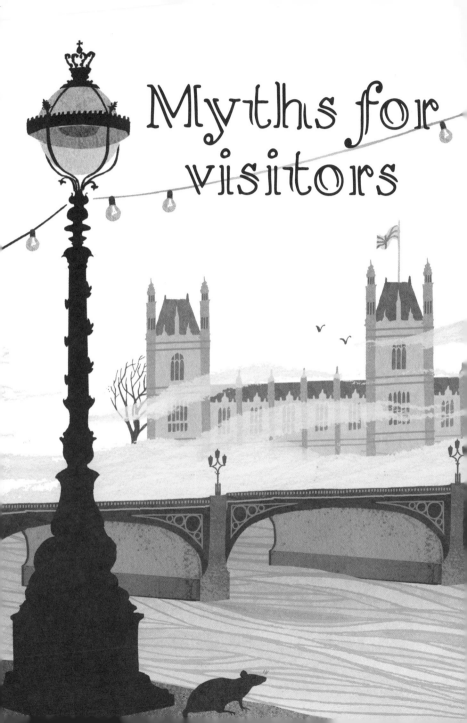

Myths for visitors

We begin with the big stuff. London's fame touches billions of people who have never visited, and never will. In forming a picture of the city, they must rely on cues from television, films, music, literature, magazines or simple hearsay. Inevitably, they get the wrong idea. To the Londoner, most of the myths in the section will be self-evidently wrong. The outsider, however, will find a few surprises.

London is a city forever shrouded in fog

London and fog go together like Rio and sun cream, or Tokyo and giant monsters. A thousand films and television programmes tell us that this is so – think Jack the Ripper, Jekyll and Hyde, Hitchcock's *The Lodger*, or the adventures of Sherlock Holmes.

Twenty-first-century London gets surprisingly little fog. Yes, we still choke and splutter on unpleasant levels of air pollution, and the city is visited by occasional patches of photogenic mist; a full-on fog that brings traffic to a halt is, however, exceptionally rare.

This was not always the case. From the beginning of mass industrialization in the eighteenth century until the middle of the twentieth century, much of London was heated and powered by coal and its derivatives. Imagine a city with millions of people, where almost every building has at least one coal fire. A colossal amount of soot was kicked up into the air whenever people needed a bit of warmth. Usually, this sooty smoke would rise and blow away in the wind. The city skulked beneath a counterpane of grime, but this did not always intrude upon the streets. Every so often, though, atmospheric conditions would collude to make what's known as a temperature inversion, where the air near the ground is cooler than that above. These inversions trapped the coal dust, leading to a thick fog at street level.

Such visitations became known as London particulars or, more evocatively, pea-soupers. This most British meteorological phenomenon was given its nickname by an American. The *Oxford English Dictionary* cites Herman Melville, author of *Moby-Dick*, with the coinage: 'Upon sallying out this morning encountered the old fashioned pea soup London fog – of a gamboge color', he wrote in 1849. (Gamboge is a deep saffron colour, most familiar from the robes of Buddhist monks.) This peculiar hue was imparted to the fog thanks to the high sulphur content in the coal smoke.* In fact, allusions to pea soup go back a few decades before Melville, with regular comparisons in minor press reports suggesting that pea soup had long been a common simile.

These dense fogs were a London phenomenon for 150 years. Their banishment was held up by two main obstacles: half-baked technology and pig-headed people. The Victorians did invent several ingenious methods for capturing and controlling smoke release, but nothing that was economically scalable to the entire city. It was not until the mid-twentieth century, when coal power began to dwindle in favour of gas and other cleaner technologies, that this problem was adequately cracked. The second sticking point was obstinacy. Whenever the Government tried to legislate against factory smoke, the wealthy industrialists would argue that their contribution to choking the nation was minuscule compared with that from the millions of domestic fireplaces. By the same token, the politician who would ban coal burning at home faced a backlash from the public. In these days before television, a warming hearth was the centrepiece of the domestic scene. Few people wanted to give up the glow and the romance of an open fireplace. It was the stalest of stalemates. Add to this a perverse fondness for the fog. It was frequently romanticized in novels of the time, and many Londoners took pride in the gloom.

Nobody could argue with the fog's detrimental effect on health, however. The final straw came in 1952, and in tragic circumstances that are often forgotten today. This was the year of the Great Smog, when a five-day blanket of pollution befouled the capital. By the standards of the time, it was a fairly ordinary fog: deep and dangerous, but not dissimilar to the visitations of previous years. Yet there was something more insidious this time. The casualties soon began to grow. The Government estimated that 4,000 people had lost their lives prematurely to respiratory illnesses in the days and weeks following the fog. That number has been revised since, and might be as high as 12,000, with many more suffering ill effects. Whatever the fatal tally, the Great Smog was almost certainly the most damaging air pollution event in the country's history. Its effects finally prompted legislation with sufficient puff to clean up the skies. The Clean Air Act of 1956 brought in smoke-control zones in city centres, promoted the use of smokeless fuels, and encouraged industrial facilities to move out of towns. Steadily, the air above London got cleaner.

In the twenty-first century, we no longer experience pea-soupers, and any kind of fog is a rare event. However, emissions from road vehicles are still a significant problem. A recent study estimated that almost 9,500 Londoners per year suffer early deaths from prolonged exposure to nitrogen dioxide and particulates in traffic exhausts. The fogs of yore might have gone, but London's air is still a killer.

---

*FOOTNOTE: If, by the way, you're wondering why a yellow fog should be named after a green dish, the answer is refrigeration, or rather the lack of it. Today, we typically make pea soup from fresh peas or those that have been frozen immediately after harvest, giving pea soup a deep green colour. City-dwelling Victorians, particularly those with little money, could not readily acquire fresh peas, and so used a dried, yellow version.

It's always raining in London

If the city is not spluttering under a heavy fog, you can bet that it's drenched in drizzle. A popular impression of London is of grey skies, sudden downpours and that inevitable break in the play at Wimbledon or Lord's.

It might be surprising to learn that London is among the driest capitals in Europe. Mean precipitation measurements vary, depending on how you take the average, but the trend is clear whichever set of data is used. In one survey, London measured 557 mm of annual rainfall, notably drier than Paris (631 mm), Dublin (758 mm), Rome (799 mm) and the sodden city of Amsterdam (838 mm). London does see more rainy days per year than some cities (109 versus Rome's 78, for example), but the overall amount is often smaller. Certainly, our reputation as a miserable and damp city is not warranted, unless you're going to compare London with somewhere on the edge of a desert, like Cairo. The capital is also the driest major city in the UK thanks to its position so far inland from the predominant south-westerly winds, which bring storms and weather fronts in from the Atlantic.

Indeed, London is in danger of becoming too dry. The South-East's large and thirsty population places a growing burden on the capital's reservoirs, to the point where the Environment Agency lists the area around the Thames as 'seriously water stressed'. In 2012, utility company Thames Water opened a large desalination plant on the banks of the Thames at Beckton - the first of its kind in the UK. Should London suffer a drought, this facility would kick into action, filtering salt out of brackish river water to provide a drinkable supply for almost a million people. It is a measure of last resort and, at the time of writing, has yet to be called into action against drought. Nevertheless, its costly construction reflects a real concern that London might run out of water if annual rainfall drops further. 'The trouble with London,' we might all grumble in 50 years, 'is that it just doesn't rain enough.'

The River Thames is filthy

'Dirty old river, must you keep rolling, flowing into the night': so crooned the Kinks' Ray Davies, in the song 'Waterloo Sunset'. The river was indeed dirty in 1967, when Ray penned those lyrics. Industrial waste and the regular dumping of sewage, particularly following damage to infrastructure during the Second World War, gave the Thames a brown, noisome character. The river at this time contained very little oxygen, and hence few creatures. It was declared biologically dead by the Natural History Museum in 1957. You would not want to bathe in it.

Around the time of the Kinks' masterpiece, a change was underway. Growing environmental awareness coupled with major investment in sewage treatment works significantly improved the quality of water. At the same time, the old, smelly industries that had characterized the Thames for centuries were in rapid decline. Fish were reported: perch, pike, roach, rudd, bream, dace and gudgeon. More exotic species arrived, such as angler fish, seahorses and even goldfish.

Then came the mammals. Seals are now relatively common in the Thames, and have been spotted as far upriver as Hampton Court Palace. Porpoises and dolphins are not unknown. Even whales are encountered in the river, with around five sightings per year. Fifty years ago, Old Father Thames rarely had a visitor. Since the river's cleansing, he's played host to 125 different species. This recuperation has not been fully appreciated by Londoners. Many do not realize that the Thames is brown from natural sediments rather than pollutants. A survey by the Zoological Society of London found that 83 per cent of Londoners, when asked to name something commonly found in the Thames, declared: 'Shopping trolley'. The river is usually clean enough for swimming, and increasing numbers are donning wetsuits upstream of Putney, where fewer restrictions are in place. Even so, there's still work to be done …

The River Thames is the cleanest major river in Europe

Efforts to clean up the river have been so successful that we now have to be careful of rowing too far the other way when describing its cleanliness. Almost any article about the modern Thames will repeat the line that it is the cleanest metropolitan river – that is, one flowing through a major city – in Europe. But is it?

This claim seems to have arisen in the 1970s, when the Thames was well on the way to recovery from its polluted past. Yet I can find no evidence in scientific literature to back up the comparison. The Port of London Authority concurs, agreeing that the claim is probably unfounded. The Environment Agency and Thames Water were also unable to supply any evidence. Such a comparison would, in any case, be tricky. What constitutes 'clean'? Which chemicals would you measure? Different rivers have different soils, climates, meanders, flow rates and native species. Any comparison would have to be hedged in caveats. All we can say is that the Thames is in much better shape than it once was, and is probably among the more healthy major rivers of Europe. It is not perfect, however.

Unlike some cities, London uses the same sewers for both wastewater and rainwater. Whenever the capital is treated to heavy rainfall, the sewers fill to capacity with a foetid soup that includes nourishing contributions from your bathroom. This feculent tide is disgorged untreated into the Thames. It has to be. The alternative would be to let our streets and homes take the surplus. This would never do, so around 40 million tonnes of tainted water finds its way into the river each year. (That figure, incidentally, is often used in a misleading way. The drains only flood during storm conditions, so that over 90% of the overflow comes from the rain. The foul matter is much diluted compared with the 'raw sewage' you'd find on a typical day's outing to a sewer. Even so, it is enough to kill fish, inconvenience rowers and give celebrity swimmers* a turn for the worse.)

This problem should soon be alleviated by the Thames Tideway Tunnel. This huge interceptor sewer will follow the course of the Thames, deep beneath the riverbed. Sewage will be diverted down into this 16-mile-long pipe, which will carry the waste to Beckton for treatment. The project, due for completion around 2022, will largely eliminate the besmirching of the Thames. Perhaps then we really will have the cleanest metropolitan river in Europe.

---

*FOOTNOTE: Comedian David Walliams was feted in the press for swimming the length of the Thames in 2011. Though not unique, it was nevertheless a remarkable achievement. Alas, the swim is chiefly remembered for making Walliams ill. His well-chronicled battle against nausea and diarrhoea did little to dispel notions that the Thames is filthy.

London is a crime-ridden city where you're likely to get mugged by an Artful Dodger type

The capital has something of a reputation for crime. Not surprising, given the long roll call of malefactors from the city's past, both real and fictional. Noted crooks include highwayman Dick Turpin, Fagin's gang from *Oliver Twist* and the Great Train Robbers. More recently, the popular imagination has been stirred by the attempted diamond heist at the Millennium Dome in 2000 and the Hatton Garden bank-vault raid of 2015. Couple this with a long history of terrorist attacks, and it's not surprising when visitors to London worry about their safety.

I've lived in London for nearly 20 years. In all that time, I've never once been mugged and only witnessed the most minor acts of criminality. One datapoint does not a pattern make, however, and we need to look at official statistics to see if London really does live up to its reputation as a dangerous place.

Comparisons between cities are not easy. Different countries use different definitions for crime, making it almost impossible to compare like with like. Furthermore, not all crime is reported, and different cities will have different levels of unreported crime. That said, we can look at a few stats that should reassure you that London is no more dangerous than any other developed city.

Let's tackle the Artful Dodger for starters. The Metropolitan Police Force*
recorded around 20,000 personal robberies in 2014–2015, which sounds like a
lot until you consider that there is a population of 8 million and an estimated
17 million tourists pass through each year.

In 2015, *The Economist* ranked the world's big cities for personal safety, using a
complex set of measurements. London came in as the twelfth most impressive
out of 50 cities, way ahead of New York, Paris and San Francisco. (The top
performers were Singapore, Osaka and Tokyo.) London was, however, trailing
New York in terms of digital security, suggesting that you're more likely to suffer
identity theft in the Big Smoke than the Big Apple.

In terms of violent crime, London certainly has its share, but no more so than
other major Western cities. The murder or homicide rate is one of the more
readily compared crimes across territories; while its definition can vary, it is less
ambiguous than, say, 'personal assault'. Using 2012 figures, the murder rate in
London stands at 1.6 per 100,000 inhabitants per year. This compared with 5.6
in New York City, 1.8 in Berlin and 4.4 in Amsterdam. More recent data shows
that London has now dropped to just 1.1 murders per 100,000.

Even within the UK, London is not always the biggest magnet for criminals.
Both Belfast and Glasgow recorded higher murder rates in 2012 (2.2 and 3.6,
respectively). In 2015, the West Midlands overtook London as the centre of
most gun crimes per capita. London suffered 19 incidents per 100,000 people,
whereas Birmingham and its environs registered 19.4. Not the most significant
difference, but illustrative that London is no worse than other big cities.

In short, a visitor to London is unlikely to become the victim of a crime,
especially if he or she sticks to the central areas. Most violent crimes occur in
residential areas away from the centre. This is not a city to fear.

---

*FOOTNOTE: The City of London Police is not included in these statistics.
However, its territory (the Square Mile) is so small that the figures would not
make much impression on the totals. It's like not including the Vatican City's
crime rate in a survey of Rome.

All Londoners speak like Dick Van Dyke in *Mary Poppins*, filling their phrases with cockney rhyming slang

'Cor blimey, guv'nor, let's 'ave a knees-up round the old joanna. Cheerio!' It's all too easy to impersonate the stereotypical cockney. The chirpy speech, wig-wagging elbows and toothy grin find their way on to our screens as regularly as those other London emblems, the hardman gangster or upper-class twit.

The cartoon cockney was most memorably personified by Dick Van Dyke, who played 'loveable chimney sweep' Bert in the 1964 film *Mary Poppins*. His London accent is, I would venture, the most ridiculed performance in Hollywood history (even if his eccentric enunciations did help the song 'Chim Chim Cher-ee' to bag an Oscar). There's no doubt, however, that the Van Dyke cockney has had a big influence on how the world sees London. Many believe that our city's inhabitants speak in that 'cheeky chappie' way. Nothing, of course, could be further from the truth. Twenty-first-century London is often reckoned to be the most ethnically diverse city on the planet. The last UK census (2011) showed that almost a quarter of London's population do not speak English as their first language, while 320,000 cannot speak English well or at all. The mayor's office states that over 300 languages are commonly spoken in the capital. Far from being a monoculture of Cor Blimey Well I Nevers, London is the most linguistically diverse place on the planet.

Most Londoners were not born in London. More than a third (36.7 per cent in the 2011 census) were spawned overseas, and probably a similar fraction moved here from elsewhere in the UK. Few, if any of these will have sufficient cockney heritage to speak like Dick Van Dyke. We might assume (though no reliable figure is available) that about a quarter of all Londoners were born in the capital. Even then, London is a big place, with numerous indigenous accents. It was once possible to tell apart a south Londoner from, say, a west Londoner, though that level of differentiation is now blurring. Aspiring middle-class types still often speak something close to 'received pronunciation' or 'the Queen's English', and this remains the most common accent in serious radio and television programming.

A growing contingent of born-and-bred Londoners speak in what is known as a multicultural London English – a dialect heavy with intonations from Afro-Caribbean cultures and other immigrant groups. Some have suggested that this has all but supplanted cockney as the working-class voice of London, to which adherents might declare, 'Oh my days!' In truth, the mix is complex and ever changing. We might happily estimate, though, that less than 10 per cent of Londoners now speak in anything approaching a traditional cockney accent. Virtually nobody uses cockney rhyming slang, except in a knowing or ironic way.

The measure of the city

What is London? The city is as slippery as its famous jellied eels. Its borders might be well defined politically, yet every Londoner has an opinion on where exactly the capital ends. Misconceptions and mistakes abound. One might even question whether London exists at all...

London is the greatest city on Earth

This is a topic endlessly debated, and one beloved of commissioning editors in search of some easy provocation. You might imagine that the statement is subjective. Either you agree that London is the greatest city on Earth, and can give multiple examples of why; or you disagree, and prefer somewhere like Paris or New York or Hull. In fact, the statement is demonstrably false, for London is not a city at all. But let's back up a bit ... You might have noticed a couple of areas of London that style themselves as cities. These are:

The City of London, also known as the Square Mile. This is the most ancient part of London, originally settled by the Romans nearly 2,000 years ago. It contains St Paul's Cathedral, the Bank of England and a growing collection of skyscrapers. It is also the smallest city in England.

The City of Westminster, which contains the Houses of Parliament, Westminster Abbey, the West End entertainment district, and various residential areas such as Pimlico and Maida Vale.

Both are officially and formally designated as cities. The City of London has been considered a city since time immemorial (as such, it possesses no charter). Westminster first dallied with city status in the sixteenth century and was granted a Royal Charter in 1900.

The two areas combined make up just 24.34 sq. km (9 sq. miles) of land – approximately 1.5 per cent of Greater London. Their joint residential population is roughly 240,000, or 2.8 per cent of Greater London. By either measure, then, the two cities are a mere trifle compared with the wider metropolis. So 98.5 per cent of London luxuriates over the remaining 31 boroughs. None of these have ever been awarded city status, although both Croydon and Southwark have unsuccessfully applied (six times in Croydon's case, which begins to smack of desperation).*

So, what is Greater London? It can be defined as an administrative area and is sometimes given the grandiloquent title of a ceremonial county, presided over by a Lord Lieutenant. It is not, strictly speaking, a city – more a collection of towns. At best, mustering the arguments from the previous paragraph, we can say it is 1.5 per cent a city. So when somebody from, say, Peckham tells you that they're tired of the city, ease their burden by pointing out that they're not technically living in one.

Londoners of a gentle disposition might now be suffering an existential crisis. But it gets worse. London does not exist at all. Not really. Yes, there's Greater London, the sprawling metropolis mentioned above. The tiny City of London also has the right to use its own officially headed notepaper. But what of plain, simple 'London'? The term has little political or formal meaning. The pedant cartographer will sketch Greater London, Inner London, Outer London, the City of London, but not London.

The term is, however, universally and firmly established as the everyday name for the sprawl of houses, roads, rails and other urban stuff that stretches out towards the M25. 'London' is used by the highest powers and organizations, including the Mayor of London, the Minister for London, the London Fire Brigade and the London Ambulance Service. In these contexts, London is more of a handle or nickname, a shorthand for the city that doesn't exist.

One of the few arenas in which 'London' does carry formal weight is in Europe. The European Parliamentary Constituency of 'London' (not 'Greater London') returns eight MEPs. I put this forward as an argument-clinching reason to vote 'No' in any referendum on leaving the European Union. If we pull out of the EU, then London will cease to exist. All that said, I'm going to use the term 'London' throughout this book for the sake of everybody's sanity.

---

*FOOTNOTE: White City and Stratford City are proper cities in the same way that Carpet World and PC World are proper planets.

The M25 is an orbital motorway that encircles London

Where is the boundary of London? Many people will tell you that the city extends out to the M25, a 188-km (117-mile) orbital road that completely engirdles the capital. Completed in 1986, the road is a compelling candidate for the frontier of the city; it appears on most maps as a striking blue boundary that divides London from all that is not London.

It is true that the M25 roughly follows the boundary of Greater London, but it does not entirely contain the city. Three small parcels of London lie outside the M25. The most significant is the hamlet of North Ockendon, at the eastern extremity of the London Borough of Havering. It survived as a quiet agricultural village before construction of the M25 cut it off from the rest of the borough in the early 1980s. North Ockendon remains a rural gibbosity, extruding beyond the motorway into Essex yet technically part of the metropolis. The two other examples are nameless and much smaller, and can be found just north of North Ockendon and over to the west near the junction with the M4.

If London occasionally seeps out beyond the M25, it also withdraws from the motorway in several places. Many populated areas that are most definitely *not* part of London can be found within the orbital. Notable examples include Watford, Borehamwood, Loughton, Chigwell, parts of Dartford, Epsom, Weybridge and Staines. A hasty, back-of-the-envelope calculation suggests around half a million people live inside the M25 but outside London.

You would also be wrong to assume that the entire route of the M25 is motorway. The 8-km (5-mile) section between Dartford (Kent) and Thurrock (Essex) is designated as the A282. This is a truly special flavour of A-road. For one thing, it trifurcates into three separate routes that pass over and under the Thames. Northbound traffic dips into either of two tunnels, whereas those heading south use the towering Queen Elizabeth II Bridge. A further oddity is that cyclists are not allowed to ride over any part of the A282. They get their own chauffeur service, albeit a highly erratic one. The Dartford–Thurrock Crossing Act of 1988 enshrines in law that anyone on a pushbike must be carried across the river for free. This sounds delightful. In reality, a cyclist must approach the crossing control along a poorly maintained cycle path, phone for assistance, and then wait for anything up to 40 minutes for a car to carry cyclist and bike over or under the river.

So, around 4 per cent of the London Orbital is A-road. Why not just make it a motorway and have a continuous and satisfying blue band right around the capital? The reasons are largely pragmatic. If the A282 were upgraded to gain motorway status, then mopeds, buses and learner drivers would not be allowed to use it. If you wanted to get between Essex and Kent in such a vehicle, you'd have to do a 32-km (20-mile) round trip to the antiquated Woolwich ferry, or even further to the Blackwall Tunnel. Keeping the crossings as an A-road is a reasonable compromise – it's just a pity they couldn't have tacked a cycle lane on to the side of the QEII Bridge.

London is the capital of the United Kingdom

London is, quite rightly, regarded as the capital city of both England and the wider United Kingdom. However, it has never formally been declared as such. It is a de facto capital, recognized by custom and tradition, but not by an official pronouncement. It has no statute or charter, or any other impressive piece of paper that might be waved in front of an international bouncer demanding to see some identification.

Nevertheless, it has been by far the largest city in these isles since the eleventh century, as well as the long-standing home of government and monarchy. (Winchester is often cited as London's predecessor as the seat of government in Anglo-Saxon times, but some historians argue that the court was effectively mobile in this period, rather than fixed near the south coast.) London may never have been formally decreed as the capital, but sometimes custom and tradition trump official paperwork. I'll leave things there as an interesting discussion point.

You have to have a London postcode to live in London

As you'll now realize, the definition of what constitutes London is subjective. One assertion is to dismiss any area that does not fall under a London postcode. If you don't live in one of the eight assigned prefixes – N, NW, SW, SE, W, E and EC – you don't live in London.

All well and good, but this excludes the denizens of Brentford, Richmond, Teddington and Twickenham (all have a TW postcode). Kingston and its KT siblings are exiled. Barnet, Bromley, Croydon, Enfield, Romford ... these entire boroughs get their marching orders. All of these places lie within the boundary of Greater London; all vote for the Mayor of London. Surely, then, all are as much part of London as the Chelsea bun? Adherents of the postcode definition would banish such places to the realms of Essex and Hertfordshire. What would they make, then, of the village of Sewardstone, just north of Chingford? This rejoices in the London postcode of E4, and yet it is most definitely in Essex.

In short, the Post Office is not a reliable authority for territorial definitions. Stick to the boundary of the 32 London boroughs for the strongest argument of what constitutes London.

London ends, and the North begins, at the Watford Gap

Those who don't drive will rarely encounter the Watford Gap. For them, it holds a near-mythical resonance: a boundary, a frontier, a huge chasm that only the foolish shall contemplate. To cross the Watford Gap is to leave the known world behind, and to pass into strange badlands signposted only as The North.

In reality, the Watford Gap is a motorway service station. It holds no fear other than the exorbitant price of a cup of coffee, the queue for the ladies' toilets and, on my last visit, a particularly petulant wasp. It lies in a shallow valley exploited by roads, rail and canal; hence the 'gap'.

The myth that the Watford Gap marks the northern limit of London is easy to explain. A glance at the Tube map shows that Watford is at the northern extremity of the Tube network. It stands to reason that the Watford Gap must be close by, and also on the northern periphery of the city. It is not. You have to travel 112 km (70 miles) farther to reach the hallowed service station, which lurks on the M1 between Northampton and Rugby. The Gap takes its name from the sleepy farming village of Watford, Northamptonshire, which – looking at Google Earth – contains a couple of dozen houses and a cow. If London ended here, it would have to subsume Luton, Northampton and Milton Keynes, and I don't think anybody wants that.

There is some sense in the idea of the Watford Gap marking a North/South boundary. While it does not guard the frontier of London, it might be thought of as a gateway to the Midlands, or the point where southern England ends.

Those living south of the Watford Gap feel the tug of London more strongly. They inhabit the satellite towns whose populations commonly commute into the capital. North of the Gap, we find conurbations that feel less of a pull from the big city. In any case, we all know Londoners who determinedly 'mind the gap' and never travel north.

The motorway service station does have an unexpectedly glamorous history. The biggest rock and roll stars of the 1960s were known to dine here while travelling to or from London on tour. The Beatles, the Rolling Stones, Cliff Richard and Pink Floyd all made good use of the Watford Gap, or the Blue Boar as it was then known. It is said that Jimi Hendrix, on first arriving in England, assumed the Blue Boar was a trendy nightclub because of its celebrity connections – although this is perhaps yet another myth associated with the enigmatic Gap.

The centre of London is at Charing Cross

In some ways this is true. Every road sign pointing to London gives the distance to Charing Cross. It can be considered *a* centre of London. But not *the* centre of London, for we have a number of problems.

First, where is Charing Cross? The station of the same name would seem a leading candidate. A visit to the station's taxi rank provides further support. Here you'll find a tall, conical sculpture, climbing from the courtyard like a Gothic space rocket. This elaborate tower of stonework is known as the Charing Cross, despite its distinct lack of cruciformity.*

The cross is a royal memorial to Eleanor of Castile. The queen of Edward I died near Lincoln in 1290. Stone memorials were built at every location where her body rested on the sombre procession back to London. The Charing Cross was the twelfth and final memorial. You can get a feel for the work of the stonemasons by heading downstairs to Charing Cross Tube station, where a series of murals by David Gentleman depicts the landmark's construction.

Look again at the monument. It is not medieval at all, but a Victorian pastiche, much more floral and overblown than the original. It is also in the wrong place. The thirteenth-century cross was built at the busy confluence of the roads to Westminster, the City and St Giles. Today, this is the annoying roundabout at the south of Trafalgar Square, a few hundred metres from the station. The roundabout itself carries the street name of Charing Cross, a detail often absent from maps (including Google Maps). So Charing Cross is the name of a station, a roundabout and a monument, all at slightly different locations – which one counts as the centre of London for the purposes of measuring distance?

It's the roundabout – or rather the statue of King Charles I that now stands at the centre of the roundabout. Charles perches on the ground occupied, until the 1650s, by the original Eleanor Cross. The medieval monument finally fell to Oliver Cromwell's purge of all things that whiffed of royalty or Catholicism. The royal absence did not last long. With the restoration of the monarchy a decade later, the equestrian statue of Charles I was erected on the site of the cross. The king still rides proud on the site today, gazing down Whitehall to the spot outside Banqueting House where he lost his head in 1649. This statue, not the train station, is the official centre of London. A plaque on the floor says as much.

Incidentally, the cross gave rise to another false fact. It is sometimes said that the name 'Charing' is a corruption of *chère reine*, French for 'dear queen'. The etymology sounds convincing, but alas the place name pre-dates Eleanor's death by at least 100 years. It is thought to derive from the Anglo-Saxon word *cierring*, or 'turning'. Both the river and the roads bend sharply at this point.

Charing Cross might be the pre-eminent locus for distance measurement, but there are other claimants to being the city's bullseye. London Stone, a forlorn piece of rock, indifferently displayed outside WH Smith's on Cannon Street, is thought by some to have marked the Roman centre. Despite making countless appearances in myth and literature (including Shakespeare), nobody knows the stone's true origins, purpose or significance. It might have been a milestone, or it might not. It was perhaps a venerated shrine to the druids, or simply a block for mounting a horse. Perhaps it was just a random piece of stone that nobody ever bothered to cart away. So much folklore has built up around that sorry piece of rock, chances are that anything you've ever heard about the London Stone is either wrong or unsubstantiated. Nevertheless, it clearly had some import for medieval Londoners, and has some claim to be the centre of their city.

A later and more historically documented candidate was the Standard on Cornhill, located where that road meets Gracechurch Street. This sixteenth-century water pump was commonly used as a datum for the country's milestones – you can still find it cited on markers such as the High Stone of Leytonstone. An echo of this role is mentioned in *Barnaby Rudge* by Charles Dickens. It was removed in 1674, when Charing Cross began to flex its centralist muscles.

Other candidates are legion. They include the church of St Mary-le-Bow on Cheapside, the hanging tree at Tyburn (Marble Arch), a now-vanished judicial building on St John Street called Hicks Hall, and a stone known as St Giles's Pound. The latter stood very close to a modern upstart, the self-declared Centre Point tower.

The heart of London can be moved at will, it seems. Perhaps we should turn to a more scientific approach. A few years ago, I decided to seek the geometric centre of London. This is an experiment you can do at home, by the way, and it's good, educational fun for children. You first need to print out an A4 map of Greater London. Paste this on to thin card – a cereal packet works well – and then carefully cut around the boundary. Now, balance the cut-out on the head of a pin or knitting needle. The point of balance is the object's centre of gravity, and therefore the geometric centre of London.

This crude method identified a location close to the Imperial War Museum. The controversial truth is that the centre of London is *south* of the river. My results were later verified by Tom Hoban, who used mapping software to pinpoint the centre of London to an accuracy of 40 cm (16 in.). His conclusion: Greet House, a residential block off Frazier Street, Lambeth. So now you know.

* FOOTNOTE: A recent April Fool's joke by city chronicler Ian Mansfield of the Ian Visits blog claimed that the protruding structure was the steeple of a long-buried church; several people were gulled, and turned up to a promised subterranean tour. The jape shows how false facts and myths are so readily introduced in a many-layered city such as London.

A true cockney must be born within the sound of Bow bells

The term 'cockney' is slowly losing its geographic identity. These days, you'll often hear it used as a synonym for a working-class Londoner from any part of town. A cockney might equally hail from Brixton, Lambeth, Camden or Hackney. A generation ago, a cockney would have suggested someone from inner east London, an inhabitant of somewhere like Whitechapel, Bethnal Green or Stepney.

Or Bow. For this is where the confusion creeps in. London has two Bow churches. One stands deep in the East End, in the conurbation known as Bow (so named because it once sported a bow-shaped bridge over the River Lea). The other is St Mary-le-Bow in Cheapside. The age-old truism that a true cockney must be born within the sound of Bow bells does not relate to the East End church, but the one in the more ancient heart of London.

How do we know? The first recorded union of Bow bells and cockneys was penned by Samuel Rowland:

I scorne (that any Younster of the Towne)
To let the Bow-bell cockney put mee downe.

This was in 1611, far too early for the area of Bow to be considered part of London and therefore cockneydom. St Mary-le-Bow, by contrast, was central to the city and, as we've seen, was commonly referenced by milestones. The word 'cockney' goes back even further. It first surfaces in the fourteenth century as 'cockeney' (meaning 'a cock's egg'), while others refer to a mystical land of Cockaigne. By Rowland's time, the term seems to have been firmly associated with Londoners.

The idea that a cockney must be born within the sound of Bow bells raises an intriguing question. How far out can the bells be heard? A study in the year 2000 estimated that in pre-industrial times, the sound of the bells might have carried as far as 9.6 km (6 miles). The pantomimic Dick Whittington memorably clocked them on Highgate Hill. Today, the chimes rarely penetrate beyond the Square Mile, thanks to a preponderance of taller buildings and the constant thrum of traffic. As there are no longer any maternity centres within that area, a true-born cockney must now be an exceedingly rare thing. At least it is still possible. In 1941, the great bell of Bow came crashing to the ground during an air raid. It was not replaced until 1961, meaning that London produced no true cockneys for two decades.

This little episode raises the corollary: how do we define a Londoner? If one needs to have been born here, then we would have to kick out our most famous citizens. William Shakespeare, please go back to Stratford-upon-Avon. Mr Charles Dickens, return to your homeland of Portsmouth. Anne Boleyn, Oscar Wilde, Samuel Johnson, Florence Nightingale, T. S. Eliot, Margaret Thatcher, Joe Strummer, Boris Johnson: return whence you came, for you are not true Londoners. Paddington Bear and Harry Potter can also clear off. And what about people like Charlie Chaplin and Alfred Hitchcock, who were born and bred in London but found most fame overseas? I was neither born in London, nor currently live in London, yet I think of myself chiefly as a Londoner. Is that allowed? Who can say? We can only fall into cliché and declare that London is a state of mind.

The City of London is a square mile

The phrase 'the Square Mile' is a useful nickname for the small and ancient central area now dominated by financial services. It is useful because its correct name, the City of London, is confusing. Not everyone is aware that the City of London, when given a capital 'C', refers to the small area of town containing St Paul's and all those skyscrapers. The city of London, when a small 'c' is employed, is a reference to the wider metropolitan area. When you say it out loud, nobody knows if you intend a small or capital 'C', and many wouldn't know the difference anyway.

Hence why the City of London is often abbreviated to just the City (itself only marginally less confusing) or, more informally, the Square Mile.

The City really did cover a square mile (well, 1.05 square miles) for much of its recorded history. But not always, and not now. In its earliest days, London was contained entirely within its city walls, like a frustrated teenager confined to her bedroom. Sure, there were settlements beyond – such as Westminster and Stepney – but these were considered as separate villages rather than areas of London. This constrained city measured roughly 1.29 sq. km (½ sq. mile).

During the medieval period, however, the City expanded to take in important approach roads. In particular, the territory was extended westward, crossing the River Fleet to encompass parts of Holborn and what is now Fleet Street. You might have seen the City dragons that mark the boundary next to Chancery Lane station, or another pair near the Law Courts on the Strand. This engorged City measured 2.71 sq. km (1 1/16 sq. miles), and lasted without alteration for hundreds of years.

Change came once again in 1994. The ancient boundaries had become impractical with evolving land use. Individual buildings, like the Ben Jonson block in the Barbican complex, found themselves straddling the boundary. Your kitchen might find itself in a different local authority to your bathroom (notionally if not practically). The course of the boundary was refined, and it now runs along the centre of roads for most of its route.

This reorganization jettisoned some ancient parts of the City while grabbing others from neighbouring boroughs. In particular, the Golden Lane Estate – a forerunner of the Barbican complex – was brought into the City. The net effect was to further swell the City into an area of land of approximately 2.9 sq. km (1⅛ sq. miles).

The City is once again threatening to spill from its bounds. Many new skyscrapers, office blocks and luxury hotels are under construction just outside the City borders in areas like Shoreditch and Spitalfields. The notion of a Square Mile feels increasingly inaccurate. In a decade, the high-rise skyline and its attendant industries will spread out well beyond the current boundary. Will the frontier be altered once again to encompass this growth? Might we soon speak of the Square Miles?

Historical bloopers

London's complex past is fertile territory for the nitpicker. As time goes on, a truth becomes an exaggeration, becomes a legend. Sometimes, new legends are invented to fit scanty facts, and the legend then becomes fact. The myths presented here are given in roughly chronological order.

Boudicca is buried beneath Platform 10 at King's Cross

One of the earliest names in London's history is Boudicca, queen of the Iceni tribe. This native Brit led a fearful campaign against the occupying Roman forces, culminating in the total destruction of London (then called Londinium) in around AD 60, along with the places we now call Colchester and St Albans.

The first item to clear up is her name. For generations, schoolchildren were taught to call her Boadicea. Then, rather recently, it switched to Boudicca. It's hard to let go of a truth that's hardwired from your schooldays, and many still cling to the name of Boadicea like stubborn charioteers. The spelling is reinforced by her statue on Westminster Bridge, beneath which the name of Boadicea is engraved, bold as brass.

Yet the earliest sources, including Tacitus (who was alive at the time of the sacking), clearly render her name as Boudicca (not just in translation, but also in the original Latin). The spellings of 'Boadicea' and 'Boadicia' were introduced in Tudor times and then popularized by eighteenth-century poet William Cowper in his 'Ode to Boadicea'. This appellation became standard until recent times, when scholars and teachers drifted back to the original sources. The *Telegraph* newspaper, ever the bastion of conservative values, still dictates 'Boadicea, not Boudicca' in its style guide.

But back to the quirky piece of trivia that heads this section. Boudicca's final resting place has long eluded archaeologists, though many locations claim her. An enduring myth places the queen beneath either Platform 9 or Platform 10 at

King's Cross station.* This outlandish suggestion was probably invented in the twentieth century, but stems from much older folklore. The name 'King's Cross' came into being in the 1830s, with the erection of a much-hated monument to George IV. Before that, the area had long been known as Battle Bridge: 'Bridge' because the now-buried River Fleet runs through the area and was spanned here, and 'Battle' because the location was traditionally associated with the final conflict in which Boudicca was vanquished. Historians do not hold much with that etymology. It is likely that 'Battle Bridge' is a corruption of 'Broad Ford Bridge' or 'Bradford Bridge'. There is no evidence that the Boudiccan battle took place here, or anywhere else near London.

Another site associated with the great queen's burial can be found a couple of miles north on Hampstead Heath. The tumulus in Parliament Hill Fields certainly looks the part of a burial mound, and it may well have been so in days of yore. It has, for centuries, been linked with the queen of the Iceni, and was even mooted as a possible site for the sculpture that now stands by Westminster Bridge. Sadly, an excavation in the 1890s yielded no evidence of interment, regal or otherwise. Other potential graves abound, from Stonehenge to Colchester. One recent and improbable conjecture points to the site of a burger chain near Birmingham – a flame-grilled whopper if ever there was one.

---

*FOOTNOTE: This has a curious resonance with J. K. Rowling's platform of choice in the *Harry Potter* stories. Juvenile wizards catch the Hogwarts Express from Platform 9¾ at King's Cross station, right where Boudicca is said to lie. Tourists will queue for over half an hour to snap a selfie at the supposed location. The Boudiccan coincidence is just that, however. Rowling has confessed that she was visualizing nearby Euston station when plotting the books: she got the station wrong.

The arms of the City of London contain the sword of William Walworth

DOMINE NOS DIRIGE

The City of London is rather fond of its shield – white and red like the cross of St George with a red sword in the upper left corner. It is pinned to the walls of many a building in the Square Mile and beyond, as well as flying from municipal buildings in flag form. But what's with the red sword?

According to legend, the device represents the weapon used to kill Wat Tyler, one of the leaders of the Peasants' Revolt of 1381. The fatal blow was struck in Smithfield by, of all people, the Mayor of London, one William Walworth. His bloody intervention ended the revolt, saving the City from mob destruction. An old and rather shaky rhyme records that:

> *Brave Walworth, knight, lord mayor, that slew*
> *Rebellious Tyler in his alarmes;*
> *The king, therefore, did give him in lieu*
> *The dagger to the city armes.*

In other words, Walworth's dagger was incorporated into the City's coat of arms as a token of thanks for his bravery. Unfortunately, the dates don't tally. The coat of arms was drawn up a few months before the peasants' uprising. It included the blade right from the start, before Tyler was slain. Most historians identify the weapon with St Paul, the patron saint of the City, who also met his end by the sword. The saint had featured on earlier versions of the arms, so this would seem a logical continuation. A document from 150 years earlier refers to a banner 'of bright red, with a figure of St Paul in gold, with the feet and hands and head in silver and a sword in the hand of the said figure'.

The sword might be Paul's and not the Mayor's, but we can still thank Walworth for ensuring its longevity on the City's arms. It was he who commissioned the redesign in April 1381, after the old version was deemed 'ill-befitting the honour of the City'.

In a final twist, the arms of London have never received formal sanction. The design was in use a century before the foundation of the College of Arms, the body that still oversees matters heraldic in most of the UK. While the shield has been 'noted' by the College, it has never been fully granted. The crest and helmet that sometimes surmount the shield, however, were finally granted in 1957.

The Great Fire of London was the greatest of all London's fires

In September 1666, it seemed to Londoners that the whole world was aflame. Samuel Pepys described the scene:

'We staid till, it being darkish, we saw the fire as only one entire arch of fire from this to the other side the bridge, and in a bow up the hill for an arch of above a mile long: it made me weep to see it. The churches, houses, and all on fire and flaming at once; and a horrid noise the flames made, and the cracking of houses at their ruins.'

The Great Fire of London, as it came to be known, certainly devastated the City of London. A population of 80,000 people lived there; 70,000 became homeless. Almost all the City's churches were destroyed, including the medieval St Paul's Cathedral. To those who bore witness, it must have felt like the greatest calamity in the City's history. In many ways, however, the Great Fire was just another of many such tragedies. London has fallen to conflagration on numerous occasions. The earliest came at the hands of Boudicca in around AD 60, less than 20 years after the founding of the Roman town. Suetonius, the Governor of Britain, had to decide where to make his stand against Boudicca's rebellion. London was not ideal as a battleground and he pulled all his troops out of the town. The city was defenceless, and the queen of the Iceni was merciless. Other fires followed. Archaeology suggests another great Roman fire in around AD 125, in which all but the most sturdy buildings were consumed. We do not know the death toll. The year 1087, in which William the Conqueror died, also saw a mighty blaze comparable to the Great Fire. It, too, destroyed St Paul's Cathedral, wrecking 'other churches and the largest and fairest part of the whole city'. The calamity was repeated just two generations later in the great fire of 1135. Fires were such a common occurrence that the medieval city must have remained as pockmarked as its disease-ravaged denizens.

The most tragic blaze occurred in 1212. It started in Southwark, taking hold of St Mary Overie (known today as Southwark Cathedral). Londoners rushed from the City on to the newly built London Bridge to lend assistance, and to gawp. Alas, the wind was up. Sparks from the fire arced across the Thames to the northern end of the bridge, where they took hold. Trapped between the two fires, the horrified onlookers succumbed to smoke inhalation, or jumped to their ends in the treacherous Thames. Later accounts put the subsequent death toll as high as 3,000. Although likely to be an exaggeration, there is no doubt that this incident ranks as one of London's worst disasters. By comparison, the Great Fire of 1666 claimed just six lives, according to official records.*

The early fires of London are mostly obscure today. We remember the 1666 conflagration partly because it was so well recorded by Pepys and others, but also because it served as the fountainhead for so much of the modern city. The cathedral and churches of Sir Christopher Wren soon arose like gleaming white phoenixes. Brick and stone replaced wood and straw as the chief building materials. The fire also accelerated the growth of what would become the West End. The fields of Covent Garden and Holborn had already disappeared beneath a tide of development. The fire served as a fillip for more house building around the periphery of the City. In the years immediately following the fire, districts such as Soho and Bloomsbury began to spread out as wealthy merchants and nobles sought new housing away from the ancient centre. Like a rose bush pruned, London must be disfigured before it can grow.

---

*FOOTNOTE: This statistic itself carries the smoky whiff of baloney. Many people fled the city, never to return. In such confusion, and with the limitations of seventeenth-century communication, it would be impossible to accurately account for everybody.

The Great Fire of London wiped out the Great Plague

This brings us on to one of the great canards in London's history. Did the 1666 fire really put an end to the Great Plague? It's a claim that's tempted educators for centuries. The timing looks perfect: everybody falls ill in 1665, then a vast, cleansing fire wipes out the disease in 1666. A neat and tidy just-so story, but correlation does not always imply causation.

For starters, the plague had eased considerably by September 1666, the month of the fire. Already by February of that year the royal court and entourage had moved back to the capital. In March, the Lord Chancellor deemed London to be as crowded as had ever been seen. When the Great Fire swept through London half a year later, it struck a city that was already well on the road to recovery. It should also be remembered that the fire only damaged the City proper. The suburbs, including plague-intensive regions such as St Giles, were completely untouched by the blaze. The fire had no direct effect on the disease in these quarters.

While the Great Fire did not wipe out the plague, it did help bring about conditions that would be less favourable to further outbreaks. The city was rebuilt to better standards, and (slightly) more sanitary conditions prevailed. These improvements were no doubt a contributory factor in keeping plague at bay in the following centuries.

A few other myths persist about the Great Plague of 1665–66. It was by no means the only disease to ravage England, nor the worst. The so-called Black Death of 1348–1350 wiped out a much higher percentage of the population – around a third of England, compared with something like 3 per cent in the 1665 outbreak. Earlier seventeenth-century epidemics, notably in 1603 and 1625, were not quite so virulent as the Great Plague of 1665, but they weren't far off. The 1665 epidemic gets more attention for several reasons: it was the last big outbreak of plague in this country; many contemporary accounts survive, unlike earlier medieval plagues; and it just so happened to occur at a time when plenty of other big stuff was going on. That the plague struck London not long after the restoration of the monarchy and just before the Great Fire of 1666 helps secure its place in our historical memory.

Finally, we can also pooh-pooh one of the most terrifying icons of the plague: the beaked helmet. Visual depictions of the disease often show sinister figures roaming the streets in these eccentric headpieces. They served as a kind of primitive gas mask for plague doctors. The beak-like appendage would be stuffed with lavender and other sweet-smelling aromatics in a bid to ward off the foul odours often blamed for the plague. Accentuating the macabre look, the doctors would also sport a broad-brimmed hat and ankle-length overcoat. A wooden cane completed the costume, and allowed physicians to examine patients without the need for personal contact. While this protective gear is well documented on the Continent, particularly in Italy, there is no good evidence that the costume was ever worn in London. It can't be entirely ruled out, but one would have thought that such a distinctive ensemble would have made it on to the pages of Pepys's diary, or some other first-hand account of the plague.

When the ravens leave the Tower of London, the kingdom shall fall

Great buildings acquire great legends. The Tower of London is a particular locus for mythology. Its ancient walls encompass at least five supposed ghosts, as well as a chest full of customs, ceremonies and tall tales. This fecund fountain of folklore has also given us the legend of the ravens. Six of the corvids must be kept at the Tower at all times; if not, the Tower will fall, and with it the kingdom.

No one is sure when the ravens became associated with the Tower. Some say that centuries of execution and gore proved irresistible to these intelligent, carnivorous birds. In the Stuart era, Tower-based astronomer John Flamsteed is said to have complained to Charles II about the constant spatter of ravens' droppings upon his telescope. 'Either the ravens go, or I go' was the ultimatum. 'You go', was the august reply, and the Astronomer Royal was packed off to Greenwich to man the now famous observatory. Or maybe the birds are hangovers from the Tower menagerie, a royal collection of animals that persisted at the Tower from the thirteenth century until 1835. Whatever their origin, the ravens have lived there since time immemorial. The Yeoman Warders, or beefeaters, jealously guard the birds, even appointing a Ravenmaster

to ensure their well-being. If they fail in their duties and the ravens escape, both the Tower and the kingdom shall crumble.

It's a powerful legend. Unfortunately, almost everything in the last paragraph is utter bilge. The yarn about fleeing ravens and falling kingdoms is younger than some of my readers. The earliest recorded mention of the legend comes from 1944, when wartime privations had seen the number of ravens dwindle to a solitary bird. As author Bora Sax opines in his scholarly paper on the subject, it is 'an invented tradition, designed to give an impression of continuity with the past'. Even the presence of the birds is relatively recent. Sax researched the topic extensively and could find no mention of any ravens in the Tower before 1895, although an illustration from 1883 includes a crudely drawn bird that might just be a raven if you squint your eyes in the right way.

I've since found a newspaper article from 1896 in which the correspondent says he's 'long heard of the Tower ravens'. He asserts that 'They were there in 1789', but gives no source. The Ravenmaster then tells the writer that the previous set of birds had unclipped wings and were prone to flying away. 'They flew to St Paul's ... and haunted the dome for months. As they were only seen on moonlit nights they occasioned a good deal of superstition.' Nothing in the article suggests that the Tower or the country crumbled as a result of the flyaway ravens.

The kingdom was also in jeopardy in 1946, when the fortress was completely bereft of the birds. The Tower had recently reopened to the public following a long closure during the war. The new intake of ravens proved difficult to tame. Four had already flown the nest or died when a fifth, called Mabel, also disappeared. The last remaining raven, Grip, vanished two months later, perhaps in search of his mate for whom he'd been pining. Two new birds called Cora and Corax were soon acquired, but not before the Tower had sustained a four-month absence of ravens. No disaster ensued, and the interlude is conveniently forgotten in every single guidebook published since.

Like human inhabitants of the Tower, the ravens have sometimes met with grisly ends. In 1947, newbie raven Macdonald was found on Tower Green without his head. Murder was suspected. Another bird, called Charlie, was despatched by a police sniffer dog in 1995. Two more were mauled by a fox in 2013.

In summary, then, the first captive ravens probably came to the Tower in late Victorian times. The legend of the fall, on loss of the birds, is almost certainly a mid-twentieth-century invention.

In ancient times, the Tower of London was regularly used to execute traitors

Despite its gruesome reputation, the Tower of London was used sparingly for executions. Most close encounters with the axeman occurred outside the fortress, on nearby Tower Hill – where today you'll find the Underground station of the same name.

In fact – and get ready to phone a friend with the news, because this one really is quite incredible – more people were executed at the Tower of London in the twentieth century than in all the other centuries put together. This counter-intuitive history can be visualised in a bloodthirsty diagram showing known executions per century.

Executions inside the Tower of London

15th	☠
16th	☠ ☠ ☠ ☠ ☠
17th	☠
18th	☠ ☠ ☠
19th	
20th	☠ ☠ ☠ ☠ ☠ ☠ ☠ ☠ ☠ ☠ ☠

Number of executions

The Tower is strongly associated with Tudor beheadings, but most executions came during the two world wars, when 11 spies were shot by firing squad within the grounds of the fortress.

For the record, here is a complete list of all 21 known executions within the Tower of London.

William Hastings, beheaded 1483
Anne Boleyn, beheaded 1536
Margaret Plantagenet Pole, beheaded 1541
Katherine Howard, beheaded 1542
Jane Boleyn, beheaded 1542
Jane Grey, beheaded 1554
Robert Devereaux, beheaded 1601
Corporal Samuel Macpherson, shot for desertion in 1743
Corporal Malcolm Macpherson, shot for desertion in 1743
Private Farquhar Shaw, shot for desertion in 1743
Carl Hans Lody, shot for spying in 1914
Karl Friedrich Muller, shot for spying in 1915
Haike Marinus Petrus Jansson, shot for spying in 1915
Wilhelm J. Roos, shot for spying in 1915

Ernst Waldemar Melin, shot for spying in 1915
Fernando Buschman, shot for spying in 1915
George Traugott Breekow, shot for spying in 1915
Irvin Guy Ries, shot for spying in 1915
Albert Meyer, shot for spying in 1915
Ludovico Zendery Hurwitz, shot for spying in 1916
Joseph Jakobs, shot for espionage in 1941

By way of parting anecdote, the roll call of prisoners at the Tower of London includes Ronnie and Reggie Kray. The troublesome twins were held for a few days in 1952 after repeated desertion from their National Service duties.* Other unusual prisoners include deputy Führer Rudolf Hess (1941) and future prime minister Sir Robert Walpole (1712) for corruption.

---

*FOOTNOTE: This nugget partly feeds my favourite pub quiz question of all time. Who are the only two people to be imprisoned in the Tower of London who also performed at the Royal Albert Hall? Answer: the Krays. A year before their Tower incarceration, the twins took part in a boxing tournament at the famous auditorium. It's another one to tell your friend, if you're phoning about that executions fact.

It was impossible to break out of the Tower of London's prison cells

Let's dispel one final misconception about the Tower of London before turning to other targets. It's often assumed that the fortress is impregnable and, by the same token, impossible to break out of. On the contrary, at least 37 prisoners have absconded from the Tower over the centuries – far more than the number executed therein. Methods have been many and varied. Some used escape ladders; one noble dressed up as a lady and walked past his misdirected guards; several internees got their keepers plastered on alcohol; bribery was also a possibility. That said, 37 escapes in 900 years isn't too shoddy – roughly one fugitive every generation.

The Tower hasn't always kept its enemies at bay, either. It was first besieged in 1191. Lord Chancellor William Longchamp was keeping an eye on England while King Richard was off crusading in the Holy Land. The national caretaker had chosen the Tower as his headquarters and set about improving the fortifications. Longchamp's fortress on the Thames attracted the envy of the king's brother, John (he who famously agreed to Magna Carta during his own tenure on the throne). Thirsty for power, John attacked the Tower. He never breached the defences, but kept up the siege until Longchamp – short of champ, with his supplies dwindling – was forced to surrender. The Tower's drawbridge was lowered, and its conqueror moved in. It would once again come under siege during John's reign, but this time held out.

One man who personifies the Tower's permeable walls is Roger Mortimer, 1st Earl of March. Mortimer was held in the Tower as a political prisoner in

1322, having led a revolt against Edward II. His treasonous lifestyle should have triggered an appointment with the executioner's axe, but instead he was given a life sentence. Mortimer would not remain a caged bird for long. A year later, he became one of the first to successfully escape the prison, via a heady combination of bribery and guard-drugging. The fugitive earl was back four years later, leading an invasion of England with the help of his lover Isabella, the queen of a cuckolded Edward II. The pair were welcomed in London, and soon captured the Tower. They went on to usurp the crown, effectively running the country until Isabella's son, the young Edward III, came of age. Mortimer again fell out of royal favour, and was thrown back into the Tower. Twice a prisoner, once an escapee and once a conqueror, the Earl had a stormy relationship with the fortress. It would be fitting to note that he was executed at the Tower but, alas, he was dispatched at Tyburn like a common criminal.

Further affronts to the Tower's defences have occurred throughout history. A mob managed to break in during the Peasants' Revolt of 1381. The Tower was comprehensively looted. The unfortunate Archbishop of Canterbury was dragged to Tower Hill and beheaded; his skull is preserved to this day in St Gregory's Church in Sudbury, Suffolk. The fortress was again besieged during the War of the Roses, and surrendered to a Yorkist army in 1460. In more recent times, the Tower took a heavy pounding during the 1940 Blitz. The last attack came in 1974, when a suspected IRA bomb detonated inside the White Tower. It killed one visitor and injured 35.

In 1671, one conniving group even came close to stealing the Crown Jewels of England, then as now housed within the Tower. The 1671 heist was led by the memorably named Colonel Thomas Blood. Having built up a rapport with the Master of the Jewel House, Blood and his cronies were able to gain ready access to the treasure. The trusting jewel master was roughed up and then stabbed, allowing the confidence tricksters to make off with a golden orb, sceptre and St Edward's Crown. They didn't get far with their ill-gotten gains. The Tower's guard apprehended the gang before they could make an exit.

You would be forgiven for assuming that the name of Thomas Blood was soon added to the list of those executed on Tower Hill. You would be wrong. In one of the great mysteries of Stuart-era England, Blood and his gang were given a royal pardon by Charles II. The ringleader was even granted some land in Ireland. Theories abound as to why the king should show such leniency, even favour, to one who had wounded several guards and almost stolen his majesty's prized baubles. Perhaps Charles was in on the plot, in some early form of insurance scam. In any case, the jewels were recovered, redisplayed and remain integral to the coronation ceremony.

Emulating Blood's feat today would be almost impossible. Forget any notions that the only thing between you and the crown is a bunch of doddery old beefeaters with blunt pikes. Every Yeomen Warder has at least 22 years' service in the armed forces. They know how to administer a sound thrashing. More pointedly, the Tower maintains a barracks of active soldiers. The jewels are at all times kept under armed guard – and that means automatic weapons, not ceremonial halberds. Finally, the jewels are kept behind shatterproof glass, 5 cm (2 in.) thick. Throw in the most sophisticated burglar alarms that money can buy and you have a jewel house that even *Mission: Impossible*'s Ethan Hunt would avoid.

Shakespeare's Globe is an accurate recreation of the original Globe

Since its rebuilding and reopening in 1997, the Globe has become one of London's most important and best-loved cultural centres. It's a close match for the playhouse that Shakespeare would have known, but not a precise copy.

For starters, it's in a different place. The original Globe was sited about 250 m (820 ft) to the south-east. A memorial courtyard on Park Street, beside Southwark Bridge, marks the spot. If we want to go even further back, the timbers that comprised the seventeenth-century Globe were originally part of an earlier playhouse – called simply the Theatre – which stood in Shoreditch until 1599, when it was spirited away to Bankside. The foundations of that theatre were rediscovered a few years ago and will be incorporated as a visitor attraction into a new skyscraper on the site, to be called the Stage.

Shakespeare's Globe also contains subtle differences to its predecessor – or, rather, predecessors. The original burned down in 1613 and was immediately rebuilt to a different design. The modern recreation is largely faithful to the pre-1613 playhouse, but incorporates several features from its replacement. The interior is entirely conjectural. We have no descriptions or images of the inside – only representations of other theatres from that period. None of this can take away from the ambience and charm with which the modern Globe is endowed.

Hitler ordered the Luftwaffe not to bomb Senate House, because he wanted to use it for a headquarters following an invasion of Britain

It was built to last 500 years. Charles Holden's art deco Senate House, part of the University of London, was the tallest block in the capital when it opened in 1937. Only St Paul's Cathedral and the chimneys of the newly erected Battersea Power Station reached higher. During the Second World War, the building served as the Ministry of Information and was later the inspiration for the Ministry of Truth in George Orwell's *1984*. It still projects authority like a stentorian headmaster.

With its stark lines, muscularity and aura of power, Senate House mirrors the work of Albert Speer, Hitler's chief architect. This helps to explain why the building is often cited as a favourite of the Führer, a potential headquarters come the invasion of London.

The building may well have drawn admiration from Hitler, but there is no record that he ever earmarked it for a Nazi HQ. It certainly wasn't avoided by the Luftwaffe. The nightly bombing of the capital during the Blitz couldn't hope to be so precise as to spare individual buildings. In any case, at least three high-explosive munitions landed within the perimeter of the complex. The tower survived unscathed.

Hitler coveted many other London buildings, at least according to 'the man down the pub'. The former Carreras cigarette factory in Mornington Crescent is one such Führer magnet. Its remarkable Egyptian embellishments once included a winged Horus emblem just beneath the roof. The effect was not unlike the eagle symbolism employed by the Nazis. It was perhaps for this reason that the sculpture seems to have been removed during the Second World War. Over time, this story probably got conflated with the Nazi HQ myth.

Or might Hitler have been eyeing up the south London area of Balham? Its Du Cane Court, like Senate House, opened in 1937 and is built in an art deco style. This large residential complex was designed in the shape of a swastika – or so a persistent rumour would have it. A quick glance at an aerial map shows that Du Cane Court more closely resembles the way a child might draw a window – four squares within a larger square. Still, its distinctive bulk might well have been used as a waymarker by German pilots approaching London from the south. Other sites occasionally linked to Hitler's ambitions include the British Museum (whose treasures he surely would have drooled over) and Whiteley's department store in Bayswater (which took a couple of Blitz hits).

Before the 1950s, London was very white and very English

Many accounts of London's history mark 22 June 1948 as a turning point. On this date, the *Empire Windrush* pulled into Tilbury Docks, a few miles downriver of London. She carried 492 passengers from the Caribbean, who would later settle in the capital. It was the first of many ships to bring Afro-Caribbeans into London, such that a decade later some 50,000 immigrants had arrived. If you believe some accounts, the *Windrush* represents a steeply angled watershed; it marks the moment when London changed from an almost entirely white English city into the multi-ethnic metropolis we enjoy today. There's no doubt that the *Windrush* did mark the start of one wave of immigration, but it was by no means the first, nor necessarily the most momentous.

London was founded by immigrants – conquering immigrants, with swords and shields and a persuasive habit of inserting a javelin into anyone who questioned their right to be here, but immigrants nonetheless. The Roman invaders built the first major settlement here from AD 43. Those founding Italians were followed by thousands of migrants, soldiers and slaves from all over their Empire. Londinium, as the Roman city was known for much of its life, became an important trading port and would have attracted merchants from all over Europe. Archaeologists have discovered items from even further afield, including objects from sub-Saharan Africa. From its earliest days, London was an international city.

And so it continued. London has always absorbed invaders, welcomed refugees and attracted economic migrants. As the Roman presence dwindled in around

AD 400, various Germanic tribes (usually labelled as Anglo-Saxons) settled in the area. These tribes were later challenged by Scandinavian groups, often generalized as Vikings. Finally, the Norman invasion of 1066 brought a strong French presence to London.

If the city's first millennium was characterized by regular settlement-by-conquest, its second was all about immigrants looking for a better quality of life. Among the most famous are the waves of Huguenots (a Calvinist flavour of Protestantism) who fled from religious persecution in France in the early eighteenth century. Some 50,000 reached England, and many settled in London. Large numbers ended up in Spitalfields and Whitechapel, and became famous for silk-weaving. You can get a glimpse of this world by visiting Dennis Severs's house on Folgate Street, a former silk-weavers' home turned into a museum.

Other continental troubles sent migrants to London. One of the greatest influxes came in the latter years of the nineteenth century. Persecution of Jews by Russia and Prussia drove refugees across Europe and to Britain's shores. By 1901, London harboured around 140,000 Jews – more than 2 per cent of the city's population. Similar numbers of Irish had arrived in the wake of the Great Famine of 1845–49. Many found work as navvies, constructing the capital's railways. By the turn of the twentieth century, London's population was a rich tabbouleh of different nationalities, with large contingents of Germans (27,000), French (11,000) and Italians (11,000).

London also has a long history of immigration from beyond Europe. There has been some kind of African presence since at least Tudor times. The population grew markedly in the seventeenth and eighteenth centuries coupled, alas, to the rise of the slave trade. Many black Londoners found employment as sailors or exotic domestic servants, though plenty of other trades were pursued. Some estimates put England's black population as high as 15,000 by the 1760s, many of whom would have lived in London.

With the abolition of slavery in 1833, fewer black people moved to the capital. The period saw an increased number of migrants arrive from Asia, with particularly large populations from India. While many lived in poverty, some were able to climb the social ladder. The House of Commons, for example, had Asian representation at a surprisingly early date. In 1841, David Ochterlony

Dyce Sombre became the first Member of Parliament of Asian descent. He was followed by the Parsi educator Dadabhai Naoroji in 1892.

Chinese workers, meanwhile, came to labour in the docks, albeit in much smaller numbers than Indian and black immigrants. A sizeable community grew up in Limehouse. It soon became famous as a hive of villainy, the home of criminals and opium dens – a reputation perpetuated by Sherlock Holmes and Fu Manchu stories. In reality, this first Chinatown was an impoverished but largely respectable place. Its seedy reputation was a sensationalist product of outsiders' prejudice and racism. An excellent counterpoint to such views can be found in the 1929 novel *Mr Ma and Son* by Lao She, which gives a Chinese perspective on London life.

The two world wars saw large numbers of foreign soldiers in London. It's an oft-repeated truth that almost a third of troops fighting for the British Empire were non-white. Many would have visited London. A similar influx was seen in the Second World War, particularly in the build-up to D-Day. During the early 1940s, the city was more ethnically diverse than at any point in its history. The arrival of the 492 men and women of the *Windrush*, at the end of that decade, can be seen as a continuation as much as a watershed. London has always been a city of diversity.

· DULWICH ·

MARYLEBONE

LEICESTER SQUARE

DEPTFORD

RUISLIP

Landmark Lies

Sometimes falsehoods hide
in plain sight. The most
famous buildings
in London are the subjects
of the biggest fibs.

The tower popularly called 'Big Ben' should actually be called 'St Stephen's Tower' – Big Ben is the bell!

The iconic clock tower at Westminster and its tintinnabulous contents are perennial favourites of pedants. '"Big Ben" is the name of the bell, *not* the tower', is surely the most common piece of nitpicking heard in the capital. 'We should not call the tower "Big Ben", but "St Stephen's Tower"', claim the same voices. When confronted with such self-assured authority, we might chant the following, in imitation of the famous bell: 'Wrong! Wrong! Wrong!'

First, it's wrong to talk of 'the bell'. There are five. A main bell and four quarter-bells.

Second, the main bell is officially known as the Great Bell. 'Big Ben' is merely a nickname given to the sonorous object in the nineteenth century.

Third, and most convoluted, we come to the tower. Many claim that the Gothic edifice is officially called 'St Stephen's Tower'. It is not, and it never has been. St Stephen's Tower is a much smaller protuberance above St Stephen's Entrance. The confusion started in the early nineteenth century, when the House of Commons sat in St Stephen's Hall. Journalists would refer to 'news from St

Stephen's' even after debates shifted to the newly built Commons chamber. The term subsequently became associated with the most iconic part of the Houses of Parliament – the clock tower.

Big Ben's tower has never carried an official name other than the Clock Tower. That is until recently. In 2012, the landmark was rechristened the Elizabeth Tower to mark the Queen's Diamond Jubilee. For the first time in the tower's existence, we now have an unambiguous, agreed-upon, official name.

I would argue, however, that the term 'Big Ben' is so intimately associated with the tower that the pedants should back away and let the popular name stand. Overwhelming public consensus confers its own form of authority, perhaps more so than an official diktat, given that we're talking about the home of democracy. So call the tower 'Big Ben' with impunity. When you're challenged by pedants, you'll be able to retort with the potted history outlined above.

It is illegal to die in the Houses of Parliament

The Houses of Parliament are part of a royal palace – the Palace of Westminster. According to ancient privilege, if you die within the palace bounds, you die in the jurisdiction of the royal coroner and are therefore entitled to a state funeral. To discourage such mischievous behaviour and its expensive consequences, long-standing legislation makes it illegal for anyone to expire within the Houses of Parliament. Quite what the punishment would be is never specified.

The whole thing is almost certainly made up. Actually, I'll stick my neck out. It *is* made up. We would be enjoying regular state funerals if this were true. Some 10,000 people hold passes to the Palace of Westminster. Along with their guests and the regular footfall of journalists, deliveries, contractors and visiting members of the public, millions of people must pass through the complex every year. By the law of averages, it is inevitable that those Gothic halls must witness the occasional death.

And they do. The most notable person to pass away was Prime Minister Spencer Perceval (1762–1812), who remains the only British PM to be assassinated. It happened in the lobby of the House of Commons. A disgruntled merchant called John Bellingham fired a pistol at the prime minister, fatally wounding him in the chest. He died almost immediately. One might also add Guy Fawkes and Walter Raleigh to the list. Both met their ends in Old Palace Yard, part of the Westminster estate. Fawkes committed suicide while awaiting execution (see below), while Raleigh was beheaded. Needless to say, neither received a state funeral.

One person who supposedly died in the Palace of Westminster but didn't is William Pitt the Elder, 1st Earl of Chatham. The esteemed statesman's final moments are depicted in a painting by John Singleton Copley called *The Death of the Earl of Chatham* (1781). The peer is shown pale and collapsing in the House of Lords, having just delivered a key speech on the American War of Independence. The implication is that he died as he lived, in the service of his country. In reality, he survived the faint and passed away 34 days later at his home in Kent. Pitt was not afforded a state funeral, but he did receive a public send-off, including a period of lying in state, and a monument in Westminster Abbey.

There are plenty of lesser examples of parliamentary demise. Does anybody recall a state funeral for Philip Wykeham Martin, MP for Rochester? He suffered a fatal cardiac arrest in the Commons library in 1878. Or Richard Tilden, guest of a Liberal MP, who fell to the floor, never to rise, outside the Harcourt Room (now the Churchill Dining Room) in 1929. Or how about James Johnston, a parliamentary journalist who collapsed and died in the press gallery of the House of Commons in 1936? In none of these cases did the press of the time raise the issue of criminality or the need for a state funeral. Nor has anyone ever produced a piece of legislation to that effect. It seems that the unlawfulness of dying in the Houses of Parliament is a recent addition to the statute book of myths.

The statue on top of the Old Bailey is blindfolded to indicate that justice is blind

The assertion that justice is blind sounds profound. In three words, one can affirm that all men and women are equal before the law. This helps explain the popular belief that the Central Criminal Court (otherwise known as the Old Bailey) is topped by a blindfolded statue of Lady Justice. The maiden is certainly up there, but with her eyes wide open and uncovered.

The bronze and gold-leafed statue is the work of F. W. Pomeroy, a renowned Edwardian sculptor who also created the four upstream figures who guard Vauxhall Bridge. She holds a pair of balanced scales in her left hand and an upright sword in her right. Trial and retribution, but no blindfold.

Misapprehensions about her optical perception are understandable. Since the fifteenth century, statues personifying justice have often been given blindfolds. Pomeroy's lady harks back to antiquity, however, when Justice was always given a clear gaze. That said, she might as well be blindfolded. Her view of Holborn and the West End was recently blocked by the lumpen New Street Square development.

A model of Napoleon's nose can be found under one of the portals of Admiralty Arch. Soldiers tweak it for luck every time they pass through

Admiralty Arch is the imposing gateway linking Trafalgar Square to The Mall. Less grandiose is the larger-than-life nose appended to one of the northern arches. Yes, it really is there. Various myths have arisen about its origins. Some say it is a spare nose for Nelson on his column, lest some confused pigeon peck it off. Another tale links it to the Duke of Wellington or his nemesis Napoleon. Sadly, it has nothing to do with Bonaparte, nor any other military figure. It's simply a piece of guerilla art, added to the Arch in the 1990s.

Around 1996, a parade of noses appeared on London buildings. Rick Butler was the mischievous artist behind the prank. His interventions, casts of his own nose, are a rebuttal to the growth of snooping technology, such as the surveillance cameras now common on the city's walls. Butler erected over

30 specimens; the West End was particularly replete with his anatomical decorations. To this day, you can still find examples on Dean Street, Bateman Street and Endell Street, among others. Another myth that has grown up around the noses is that whoever finds them all will achieve infinite wealth. Perhaps for this reason, tour guide Peter Berthoud now leads the nasally curious around the 'Seven Noses of Soho' on regular tours. He is not, as far as I can judge, infinitely wealthy.

Butler's project had its imitators. A much larger protuberance appeared at the eastern end of Meard Street in Soho about a decade ago – its erector did so independently of Butler's project, using a cast-off nose from a replica of Michelangelo's *David*. A set of tiny white fingers could once be seen on the wall of Phoenix Garden near Charing Cross Road. Meanwhile, artist Tim Fishlock recently engaged in a copycat project with ears instead of noses. You can still find a couple of his aural sculptures on Floral Street in Covent Garden, where the walls literally have ears.

If the Union flag is flying on Buckingham Palace, it means that the monarch is at home

Stand outside Buckingham Palace for two minutes and you're sure to hear a tourist make this claim. The reverse is true. A fluttering Union flag indicates that the monarch is *not* currently in residence. A Royal Standard is the flag to look out for. This is the red, yellow and blue affair that unites the excessively stretched lions of England, a rampant rouged lion to represent Scotland, and an Irish harp of lewd profile (take a close look). This flag, technically a banner of arms, flies over any building lucky enough to accommodate the Queen, so long as it has a flagpole.

The death of Diana, Princess of Wales in 1997 sparked this particular confusion. Before that time, the Royal Standard was the only flag commonly raised and lowered above the palace. It was a simple matter to determine whether the Queen was at home: flag = yes, no flag = no.

In the days following the tragedy, the Royal Household found itself in a bit of a quandary. Public feeling demanded that a flag be flown at half mast in respect. The Royal Standard, by tradition and the logic of inheritance, cannot be flown at half mast because the sovereign never dies.* The Queen, who was absent from the palace at the time of Diana's death, decided to break with tradition and fly the Union flag at half mast. This protocol now applies for any royal death or period of national mourning (including, controversially, the death in 2013 of Margaret Thatcher). The red-white-and-blue is now also flown at full mast whenever the monarch is away from Buckingham Palace, meaning that the flagpole is never bare.

---

*FOOTNOTE: The new monarch instantaneously succeeds his or her predecessor, making royal succession one of the few things that can travel faster than the speed of light.

Old London Bridge was sold to a gullible American who thought he was buying Tower Bridge

Every Londoner has been asked for directions to 'the London Bridge'. The mischievous among us dutifully direct them to that nondescript river crossing, knowing full well that they're really after Tower Bridge. If the city coffers got a pound for every time a tourist mixed up the two spans, we wouldn't need to pay council tax.

The ultimate fall guy in this respect is one Robert P. McCulloch. This US entrepreneur bought an earlier version of London Bridge in the 1960s. Like many an American since, however, McCulloch got his bridges mixed up and thought he was purchasing the much more decorative Tower Bridge.

That, at least, is the myth that went along with the sale, and still gets bandied about today. There is no evidence that McCulloch was mistaken – he knew what he was buying. Travis Elborough, in his magnificent 2013 book about the sale, *London Bridge in America*, devotes a whole chapter to exploring this legend. He points out that the City of London prepared a detailed brochure for the bridge, the merest perusal of which would leave the potential buyer in no doubt which span was for sale. For Elborough, the clinching evidence came in a contemporary radio interview with McCulloch's son, Robert. Asked if his family had its eyes on any other British landmarks, Robert Jr. quipped that he'd had some talks with the City about purchasing Tower Bridge, though they weren't playing ball – understandably given that Tower Bridge had become a totemic emblem of the city, present on a thousand postcards.

Elborough posits that this interview might have kick-started the myth. Through a process of Chinese whispers, a joke about buying an iconic structure was gradually transformed into an embarrassing case of mistaken identity. The notion ties in with British prejudices about our 'dim American cousins'. As Elborough points out, the McCulloch story is a convincing twist on a whole genre of urban legends about unscrupulous crooks posing as agents of the Crown and selling landmarks to naive tourists.

In any case, McCulloch seemed happy with his purchase. The bridge was shipped over to Arizona, stone by stone, and re-erected in Lake Havasu City. It stands there to this day as a tourist attraction, and the world's largest sold antique. If you want to see the displaced structure in all its Technicolor glory, seek out the awkwardly titled *The Special London Bridge Special* (1972). This stupendously daft movie-cum-advert sees Tom Jones (as himself) crooning his way around Lake Havasu City in the company of such improbable guest stars as Kirk Douglas, Charlton Heston, Rudolf Nureyev and the Carpenters. The implication is that London Bridge retains its magic, even in this new home. The reality is a film so hammy, you'll want to smother it in mustard.

Incidentally, it would be wrong to assume that all of London Bridge was transported to America. The sale comprised mostly balustrades, stone cladding and other surface materials – in effect, the outer shell of the bridge, which was then rehung on a fresh structure in Arizona. A large section of the bridge's approach was maintained on the Southwark side of the river, including the arch that is home to the London Bridge Experience (see 'Nancy's Steps' in the 'Plaques That Got It Wrong' section).

The Shard is the tallest building in Europe

Here's a fact for you: the Shard skyscraper is almost exactly six times the height of Nelson's Column (308.5 m/1,012 ft versus 52 m/170 ft). It is the tallest building in the United Kingdom. It is not, as often claimed, the tallest building in Europe. Three towers in Moscow trump it, the tallest of which is the 374-m (1,227-ft) Federation Tower. Moscow can boast eight of the ten tallest buildings in Europe, with only London's Shard and Frankfurt's Commerzbank Tower jockeying for position in the high-rise league. It would be accurate to say that the Shard is Western Europe's tallest building, or else that it is the tallest building in the European Union.

Now, I said up top that the Shard is the tallest building in the UK. However, it is not the tallest artificial *structure*. Not by a long way. 'Buildings' are defined as 'objects with habitable floors' – spaces through which you can walk, and exclaim 'Coo, what a view.' Structures, by contrast, do not need to have floor plates. Think of a flagpole, an obelisk or a communications mast. If we include these, the Shard ranks as only the tenth-tallest structure in the country. The lofty crown goes to Cumbria's 365-m (1,197-ft) Skelton Mast.

Counterfeit buildings

Sometimes the very bricks and mortar of London deceive. You may think that you are looking at a building, or a sculpture, but you are wrong. A much-noted example can be found in Leinster Gardens, near Notting Hill. This gleaming white row of houses appears to extend uninterrupted for the length of the street. What many passers-by fail to clock are the fake houses at numbers 23 and 24. Although a perfect match for neighbouring properties, with a full complement of windows, balustrades and doors, the twin homes are just facades. The empty houses were constructed in the 1860s to conceal a gash in the terrace, hewn out for the construction of the District Line beneath. You can undermine the illusion by walking round the corner to Porchester Terrace for a peek over the railway wall. From this vantage point, it is clear that the Leinster Gardens houses are merely a front. Even simpler, visit the location on Google Earth and you can view the deception from multiple angles.

These hollow neighbours have attracted their mythologies. It's commonly written that local pizza companies induct new drivers by getting them to deliver to the impossible addresses, or else are sent there by jape-making callers. Tube journalist Andrew Martin investigated the twin non-properties in the 1990s. Paying a call to the guest house next door, he discovered that the proprietor had no idea he worked beside a fake house. The street gained renewed fame a few years ago, when the terraces featured in an episode of the BBC's *Sherlock* series. (The writers cleverly played upon the title of an original Conan Doyle story called *The Empty House*.)

While Leinster Gardens offers the most peculiar instance of fakery, it is not the only sham structure in London. A highly visible example is under construction in Nine Elms as I write. The four chimneys of Battersea Power Station are undergoing demolition; unsafe, so they say. They will be replaced by four exact replicas – a story that will be all over the news for a few weeks before slipping from public consciousness. A decade hence, most will assume that they are part of the original fabric of the building.

The City of London contains many remakes. More or less any Christopher Wren church is a hybrid of original early eighteenth-century stone and twentieth-century makeover. Churches such as St Giles Cripplegate (Barbican) and St Mary-le-Bow (Cheapside) suffered almost total destruction to their naves during the Second World War. Their towers are often original, but the main bodies of these churches are skilful recreations.

Ventilation shafts afford a special class of trickery. Any sizeable tunnel needs some kind of duct to allow fumes to escape, and to aid the circulation of fresh air. Simple pipes or concrete boxes will often do the job, but some London vents are hidden in plain sight. The garden of Gibson Square in Islington offers one example. Here, a classical-style brick building looks like a Victorian shelter. The truth is revealed when you notice the metal-mesh roof – this is a flamboyant ventilation shaft for the Victoria Line, built in the 1970s. London's grandest vent serves the Piccadilly road underpass. When the subway was built in the 1960s, one side of the Wellington Arch was fitted out to serve as a flue. Other prominent examples include the mock-Tudor hut in Soho Square, the classical column in Paternoster Square, a metallic sculpture by Sir Eduardo Paolozzi next to Pimlico station, and the ticket booth at the south of Leicester Square, which ventilates a little-known electricity substation beneath the garden.

Finally, Tower Bridge contains a hidden chimney. Look on the northern side of the bridge, just as it reaches land, over by the Tower of London. One of the cast-iron lamp posts is of a different design to the others. It is an imposter, shedding no light but instead helping to expel smoke from an old fireplace within the Tower grounds, long since extinguished by the Clean Air Act.

A statue of Eros stands in Piccadilly Circus

Eros has been hailed as the most famous statue in London. Only Nelson can compete, and he's more admired for his massive column. Yet the winged sculpture in Piccadilly Circus does not, strictly speaking, depict Eros. And contrary to what you might read in other London trivia books, it might not depict any particular supernatural being at all.

The sculpture was unveiled in 1893, the crowning glory of a monument to the 7th Earl of Shaftesbury. It takes the form of a bronze ornamental fountain, topped by the enigmatic aluminium statue, reputedly of Eros.

In truth, the statue didn't really take on any kind of identity or iconic status until the early twentieth century. Until then, the monument was usually referred to as the Shaftesbury Memorial Fountain (despite its erratic, often non-existent water supply). Nobody really had a clue about the identity of the winged figure. A poll conducted in 1914 by a Mr Sigismund Poetz found that 42% of people thought the statue depicted the god Mercury; 29% didn't know; 13% thought it was 'some kind of genius'; 11% assumed it was a female figure; while only 5% believed it to be Eros (the correct answer, according to Mr Poetz). Another account five years later reckoned that 'Many people believe it to be of Hermes' – the Greek equivalent of Mercury.

In recent years, the figure has been increasingly identified with Anteros, the twin brother of Eros, and the god of requited love. No press reports of the time mention this dedication. In any case, nobody's ever heard of Anteros. The name has never stuck, except among pedants who wish to score an easy point against those who think it's Eros.

Indeed, Alfred Gilbert was always coy when it came to associating his sculpture with any particular deity. Writing in 1903, a decade after the unveiling of the fountain, he admits the figure is more an idealized embodiment of Shaftesbury:

'If I must confess to a meaning or a *raison d'être* for its being there, I confess to have been actuated in its design by a desire to symbolize the work of Lord Shaftesbury; the blindfolded Love sending forth indiscriminately, yet with purpose, his missile of kindness, always with the swiftness the bird has from its wings, never ceasing to breathe or reflect critically, but ever soaring onwards, regardless of its own perils and dangers.'

Gilbert was retrospectively justifying his work after various attacks in the press. One correspondent to *The Times* deemed the flighty, arrowless and nude figure 'not only intensely ugly in itself, but it is at the same time a gross libel upon the deceased'.

The statue has alternatively been dubbed the 'Angel of Christian Charity'. One story, which seems to have taken root on Wikipedia without citation, asserts that the overt depiction of free love, in the form of a naked youth, was all a bit much for Victorian prudishness. Transfiguring the dashing inamorato into an angel of charity would better reflect the sober, respectable Earl of Shaftesbury. Gilbert's explanation that the statue embodies Shaftesbury's selflessness seems to have led others, observing the wings, to invent the Angel of Christian Charity identity.

And so the figure on top of the fountain remains officially nameless. The overwhelming majority of people now know it as Eros. As with the nickname 'Big Ben', such popular consensus carries its own weight of authority. Let's just call it Eros.

The monument is associated with other myths. It is often noted that Eros draws back an empty bow. This pose serves as a rebus, or visual pun, for his missing shaft is buried on Shaftesbury Avenue. Alas, our muddled archer does not face along that road, and never has done. This one, too, was probably made up after the event, although it's entirely possible the sculptor had it half in mind when designing the piece.

Finally, Eros has not always presided over Piccadilly Circus. Between 1924 and 1931, he was placed on a concrete stand in Embankment Gardens while his usual home underwent major construction work for a new tube station.

Green Park contains no flowers, on the order of Queen Catherine of Braganza

Of all the Royal Parks in central London, Green Park carries the most descriptive name. It is a relentlessly verdant affair almost exclusively populated by plane trees and grass. Contrary to popular belief, however, it does contain plenty of flowers. The visitor of early spring is welcomed by a carpet of daffodils, particularly in the south-east corner, where the golden host complements the richer plantings at the foot of Constitution Hill.

What Green Park does lack is formal flower beds. No recently upturned earth or neatly trimmed borders here. All flowers in Green Park rise from an ocean of grass. The reason for the lack of flower beds is lost in the mists of time, although a charming myth seeks to explain the absence. It is said (usually by tour guides) that the flower beds were filled in during the seventeenth century on the orders of Queen Catherine. The feisty wife of Charles II had spotted the Merry Monarch plucking flowers here for his mistress. In a fit of pique, she ordered that the park should never blossom again. It was forever after called Green Park to reflect the lack of inflorescence. If you want to delight your loved one today, you must settle for daffodils or dandelions.

There's no way to disprove this floral tale, but it seems unlikely. References to the legend are few and far between until the twenty-first century, which makes me suspect that this is a modern-day invention for the sake of the tourist dollar.

We do know that the open space was originally called Upper St James's Park, but changed to the Green Park around 1746, long after Charles II's time. Maps from the era, such as that of John Rocque, show the land as largely open with few trees. It has always stood in contrast to the more managed spaces of the neighbouring parks. An early Victorian commentator described the Green Park not as green, but 'very rough, weedy, brown, battered, open space, where people of by no means pretty behaviour were wont to resort at all hours of the day, and some hours of the night'. It is much more gentle today, especially if you shy away from the noisy Piccadilly end.

The missing flower beds might be seen as sympathetic of London as a whole. The city is a concrete jungle, where nature is dislodged by tarmac and any greenery is restricted to the heavily managed royal parks. Such impressions are common among Londoners and visitors who don't pay much attention to their surroundings*. If we open out eyes, though, London is teeming with life. Street trees are everywhere – some 70,000 can be found in Westminster alone, including the mighty London plane trees that dominate the wider roads and central parks. Mighty thoroughfares like Kingsway and Aldwych appear as linear jungles when viewed from above (take a look at an online satellite view if you don't believe me). As we move out into the suburbs, an increasing amount of land is given over to plants and animals. According to one estimate, a staggering 8.3 million trees call London home. If you include the many forms of insect and aquatic life, some 13,000 species share our city. The killer statistic, however, is that nearly half the land (47%) in Greater London is physically green. Such revelations have prompted a campaign to designate London as a 'National Park City', putting it on a similar footing to the New Forest or the Yorkshire Dales.

---

*FOOTNOTE: Or, perhaps, those who never leave Fitzrovia – a district that, as far as I can tell, has only one patch of public grass. Soho isn't much better.

The prime meridian passes through the Royal Observatory, Greenwich

Any first-time visitor to the observatory at Greenwich may indulge in straddling the meridian line. The stainless-steel marker runs along the top of the slope leading to the observatory buildings. A typical visitor will examine the line for a few seconds and then jump back and forth across the line, usually with big grin on his or her face. The clever tourist has mastered both time and space, and can leap from eastern to western hemispheres in a single bound.

The line continues to the observatory itself, where it runs up the face of the building used by George Airy to determine the meridian in 1851. Since 1999, the meridian has also been marked by a green laser, which beams out of the Airy building during the hours of darkness. Unfortunately, both laser and marker are in the wrong place. The true Greenwich meridian lies to the east.

You can see this for yourself. If you take an accurate Global Positioning System (GPS) reader to the supposed meridian line, you'll note that it does not read precisely 0°0'0' as expected, but is ever so slightly out of kilter. The reason? Better technology. Airy's technique was relatively primitive. He measured what he thought was a perfectly horizontal baseline using a bowl of mercury. The liquid's surface is exquisitely flat. One can then measure the perfect perpendicular to this surface – that is, a line running upwards to a point directly overhead, and down to the exact centre of the Earth. With these baselines fixed, Airy could calculate a true north–south line to the poles. This became the official Greenwich meridian, and passed straight through the Royal Observatory. It was later adopted internationally as the global standard for navigation.

Alas, Airy's technique was not precise enough. The first geostationary satellites noted a small discrepancy in the angle of the line. If one of those prancing tourists decided to follow the meridian marker down the hill, across the water to the Isle of Dogs, and on towards the realm of the polar bears, he or she would find themselves ever so slightly offset from the true North Pole. Airy's bowl of mercury was a flawed device. The Earth is not a perfect sphere, but bulges at the centre. Local geology can also cause small deviations in the planet's gravitational pull. The effects combine to make Airy's technique imprecise – although impressively close given his technology.

We're only talking a few metres here. However, global positioning satellites are sensitive enough to spot the difference. Since the 1990s, the official Greenwich meridian has lain 102.5 m (336 ft) east of the tourists' line, and does not pass through any of the observatory buildings. As yet, there is no marker or plaque denoting this line.

The BT Tower has no stairs, and is the only building in Britain that may evacuate using lifts in an emergency

The BT Tower has dominated the skies of Fitzrovia for half a century. It was opened in 1965, as the Post Office Tower, to serve as a communications relay mast. Its pencil-thin profile has led to rumours that it lacks a stairwell, with room only for a lift shaft. The hundreds of charity fundraisers who climb the 842 steps to the top each year might wheezily dispute this claim.

The tower does indeed have special dispensation to evacuate by lift, but it is not the only building where this is the case. The Shard and Heron Tower, for example, both have dedicated fire lifts. This is now standard practice for many tall buildings, though the BT Tower might have been among the first to adopt it. You may have read that the BT Tower was, until recently, classified as an Official Secret. The structure was used to relay military and governmental communications, making it a potential target for the nation's enemies. Taking photographs of the tower was illegal, and it was left off public maps until recent times. This all has a dubious ring about it. The tower was and remains one of the tallest structures in London, and is particularly prominent in the otherwise flat neighbourhood. It has featured in numerous films and television programmes, and even on postcards. A public restaurant, famous for rotating to give diners a 360° view of London, operated from the upper floors for the tower's first 15 years. It is scarcely possible to conceive of a more noticeable 'secret'.

This curiosity came to light in 1993, when Kate Hoey MP raised the matter in the House of Commons. She noted that the tower was absent from Ordnance Survey maps. 'I hope that I am covered by parliamentary privilege', said she, 'when I reveal that the British Telecom Tower does exist and that its address is 60 Cleveland Street, London.' The statement is puzzling. A glance at a 1970s OS map clearly shows the complex, labelled as 'Telephone Exchange & Post Office Tower' in a bold typeface. An A–Z map of the same era also shows the Post Office Tower, while a copy from the late 1980s employs a prominent black dot beside the tower's name. A third map, the London Street by Street atlas from the mid-1970s, also shows the tower. In fact, I've been unable to track down a single map that lacks the landmark. Even a Bartholomew's atlas from 1961, four years before the structure was complete, marks the 'PO Radio Tower'. Hoey's statement notwithstanding, the whole story appears to be a fiction.

In 1971 a small bomb exploded on the 31st floor of the tower. It is often said that the device was planted by the IRA, and its detonation brought an end to public access. Neither observation is entirely accurate. Although the IRA would seem to be the obvious culprit, there had been no recent precedent. It had been more than 30 years since the last republican bomb in England, and a renewed campaign of violence would not begin until two years later. Instead, the Post Office Tower blast is often attributed to a left-wing anarchist group. An anonymous caller – 'well spoken with an English accent' – phoned the Press Association shortly after the bombing. He claimed that the attack had been the work of a group called the Angry Brigade, in protest at the Government taking the country into the Common Market.

Some confusion remains, however. It's often stated today that the IRA made no claims for the attack. Yet newspapers of the time reported a call from a man with an Irish accent claiming responsibility for a Kilburn unit of the IRA. The anonymous caller threatened to detonate his next bomb at the Victoria Tower of the Houses of Parliament, an attack that never materialized. The true culprits remain unknown, at least in the public record. In any case, the rotating restaurant reopened three weeks after the blast, but quickly went out of business. The space is still largely off-limits today, although regular functions and charity climbs offer some form of access – and proof that the stairs really do exist.

Famous Londoners

The cult of celebrity generates
its own myths. Common
outlaws become heroes,
while genuine heroes become
pantomime characters. Here,
we look at some of the untruths
told about the more notable
London personalities.

Dick Whittington was a lowly farmer's boy who became Lord Mayor of London three times, with help from his cat

Dick Whittington was London's first superstar. We all learn his story as children. Dick starts out as a poor country bumpkin, orphaned and alone. He is enticed to London by the legend that its streets are paved with gold. Instead, he finds only servitude and misery. His only comfort is the pet cat he has acquired for a penny. Frustrated with his lot, Dick flees the city. His cat, meanwhile, takes to the high seas as a ship's mouser. While climbing Highgate Hill, Dick is stopped in his tracks by the sound of Bow bells. 'Turn again Dick Whittington, three times Lord Mayor of London', they chime. With new resolve, our young hero returns to the city. He discovers that he has become a rich man thanks to his trusty cat. The plucky feline had served well, ensuring the profits of her ship. Dick takes a share in those profits and goes on to become the leading citizen of the town. Just as the bells prophesied, he becomes Lord Mayor of London three times. Everyone lives happily ever after.

The legend of Dick Whittington lives on in pantomime and children's books. The story is loosely based on the life of Richard Whittington (*c*.1354–1423). Far from starting out as a poor country lad, the genuine Dick came from a prominent Gloucestershire family. His grandfather William Whittington had been knighted and his father owned large estates. Nevertheless, Richard, as a younger son, would not inherit this land and was encouraged into trade. He travelled to the City of London, where he joined the Mercers' Company. In time, he became a stupendously successful merchant, selling fabrics to the royal court and wealthy overseas buyers. He served as Lord Mayor of London on four occasions, not three, and also found time to be Mayor of Calais and a Member of Parliament. He was also a great benefactor to the City. His munificence funded the rebuilding of the Guildhall, a ward at St Thomas's Hospital for unmarried mothers, several drainage systems and the Whittington Longhouse, a mega-toilet with 128 seats (64 for men and 64 for women).* Small wonder that his story has lived on, first in ballads and pamphlets, and later on the stage.

But did he have a cat? No primary evidence exists to prove it, but nor can it be ruled out. References exist to a near-contemporary painting and statue of the great man, both of which supposedly incorporated a cat. They have long been lost, however. As if to further cement the legend, a 1949 search for Whittington's tomb at St Michael Paternoster Royal failed to find the Lord Mayor, but did uncover a mummified cat. Later analysis dated the remains to Christopher Wren's rebuilding of the church in the late seventeenth century.

Today, you can find at least four public works of art devoted to Whittington or his cat. A statue of the pair lurks beneath the arches of Guildhall Art Gallery in the City. Nearby, a painted Dick climbs the steps leading up to the Museum of London; his faithful pet races ahead on the floor above. Another statue of Dick (minus cat) guards the northern face of the Royal Exchange. A final feline simulacrum can be found outside the Whittington Hospital on Highgate Hill. It perches on a much older stone, said to mark the spot where Dick heard the sound of Bow bells.

---

*FOOTNOTE: A contender for the world's first public toilet. Why no enterprising tour company has recreated this unique landmark is beyond me.

Guy Fawkes was executed for masterminding the Gunpowder Plot

Every year, thousands of people make life-sized effigies of a Catholic Yorkshireman, then set him on fire for the delight of their children. Guy Fawkes is such a bogeyman that his annual immolation has yet to be quashed by newspaper columnists and other self-appointed guardians of morality. This is the man who plotted not just to bring down the system, but to blow up the king and his government too. In 1605, his actions were branded as treachery and treason. Today, we would call him a mercenary or terrorist. But does Fawkes truly deserve the animosity of centuries?

His story is well known to every British schoolchild. Guy Fawkes, real name Guido Fawkes, was angry at the state for its anti-Catholic prejudice. He brought together a team of conspirators intent on killing King James and his cronies during the State Opening of Parliament. Under cover of night, they broke into the House of Lords and loaded the basement with barrels of gunpowder. The plot was discovered, however, on the eve of success, thanks to an anonymous tip-off. Fawkes was arrested, tortured and eventually gave the names of his auxiliaries. All were eventually captured and executed.

The story is wrong in almost every respect. Fawkes was not the ringleader. He was merely the first to be captured when the guards caught him red-handed and alone in the gunpowder cellar. The true mastermind was Robert Catesby. He led the team of 13 conspirators – Fawkes had no special place in the hierarchy, but was chosen to light the fuse at the assassination attempt. Nor was he born as Guido. That was a nickname he adopted while fighting for the Catholic Spanish in the Eighty Years' War. His birth name was plain old Guy.

The conspirators did not break into the Houses of Parliament. In fact, they took out a lease on the undercroft and had lawful access to the space. The gunpowder stash was built up over a number of days, and four months before the plague-delayed opening of Parliament on 5 November.

Fawkes did indeed receive the death penalty for high treason, and was dragged to the gallows in Old Palace Yard to be hanged, drawn and quartered. This terrifying procedure would first see the condemned man dangle by the neck until barely conscious. After being cut down, his genitals would be sliced off and his belly opened. His entrails would then be scooped out and burnt with his testicles. Finally, the fading man would be chopped into parts, which would, in a gory sequel, be displayed in public locations as a warning to others.

It didn't quite happen like that. Before the executioner could begin the gruesome act, Fawkes leapt from the gallows, breaking his neck and sparing himself the excruciating fate the law had set out for him. In short, he was not executed, but committed suicide. Other conspirators also escaped the chop. Ringleader Robert Catesby and several others were killed in a gunfight with authorities in Staffordshire, while a further plotter died from illness at the Tower of London before he could stand trial.

Dick Turpin was a dashing highwayman who rode from London to York in one day

Few figures in London's history attract as much embellishment and fabrication as Dick Turpin. The exploits of the infamous highwayman have been much romanticized over the years, and it is difficult to separate the myth from the man.

The popular image of Turpin was shaped largely by William Harrison Ainsworth in his novel *Rookwood*. Published in 1834, almost a century after Turpin's execution, the story weaves a fictive cloak around the highwayman. Turpin is only a secondary character in the story, but nevertheless looms large and glamorous, eclipsing the wobbly stereotypes who make up the main cast. His dashing ride to York is particularly well realized. Trusty mare Black Bess accomplishes the 322-km (200-mile) flight in less than a day (the stagecoach took four days), before dying of exhaustion at the edge of that city. 'Gone, gone! and I have killed the best steed that was ever crossed! And for what?', cries Dick.

For a great deal, it turns out. The fictitious ride to York cemented the Turpin legend in the popular imagination. He is now so established as an archetype that few people could name any other highwayman.

The truth is very different. Turpin operated as a highway robber for just four years, following a longer career as a housebreaker and thief. Even then, press reports unequivocally linking him to highway hold-ups are scarce, and he was eventually convicted for horse theft.

Turpin was just one of many mounted robbers to terrorize the open road. Earlier rogues such as James Hind, Claude Du Vall and John Nevison enjoyed popular fame from the seventeenth to nineteenth centuries, but are today largely forgotten. Their stories somehow became entangled with Turpin's. Du Vall, for instance, was renowned for his gentlemanly behaviour when holding up a stagecoach. Nevison, meanwhile, was the original fast rider. His (probably apocryphal) 322-km (200-mile) dash from Chelmsford to York inspired Turpin's flight in Ainsworth's *Rookwood*.

Black Bess is a fiction. As a noted horse thief, Turpin no doubt galloped on many a fine steed, yet there is no record that he ever favoured one particular mare. The name 'Black Bess' is probably a nineteenth-century invention, taking hold in pamphlets and other ephemera before establishing its place in the Turpin canon through *Rookwood*. No horse can travel 322 km (200 miles) in one day under its own power.

Turpin himself was probably a thuggish, unattractive man. No contemporary illustrations exist, but a few descriptions were made in the newspapers. One 1737 account essays a character 'about five Feet nine Inches high, of a brown Complexion, very much marked with the Small-Pox, his Cheek Bones broad, his Face thinner towards the Bottom, his Visage short, pretty upright, and broad about the Shoulders'. He murdered on at least one occasion and was implicated in many savage beatings. Far from being the gentlemanly desperado of legend, Turpin was a pockmarked delinquent.

Still, his legend began in his own lifetime with the publication of ballads of derring-do. Soon, the Turpin story was a regular on the stage. By the early nineteenth century, his legendary ride to York had become established 'fact'. Ainsworth's 1834 novel brought it all together in a popular work of fiction, whose influence is still with us today.

Many London pubs claim Turpinic connections. Chief among them is the Spaniard's Inn, beside Hampstead Heath. It's often claimed that the inn was a regular haunt of the highwayman. A sign outside the pub even asserts that Turpin's father was once landlord of the Spaniard's, and that his errant son was born here. As a child, Dick would watch the passing coaches from an upstairs window, plotting out his future career. There is no evidence for any of this. To the contrary, records survive to show that Turpin was christened in the Essex village of Hempstead. It looks like a case of Hampstead/Hempstead confusion, exacerbated by the fact that other highwaymen were active around the Hampstead area. There is even some doubt as to whether the Spaniard's Inn existed during Dick's lifetime. The fabric of the building is certainly old enough, but several unsupported sources say that it was not used as an inn until several years after the robber's death.

Nevertheless, the Spaniard's Inn plays up to the legend. It has a Turpin room, and has a long history of displaying fake Turpin relics. In the early years of the twentieth century, drinkers could marvel at the sword with which the highwayman killed his last victim. 'Observe', read the label, 'the bloodstains on the blade.' No record exists of Dick Turpin stabbing anybody. The pub also displayed part of the tree upon which the malefactor was hanged. Alas for authenticity, Turpin was executed on York's gallows, not a tree. In more recent years, visitors could examine the highwayman's pistols. Ironically, these appear to have been stolen.

Sweeney Todd was the demon barber of Fleet Street

On Fleet Street, close to where the cities of London and Westminster kiss, can be found a narrow passageway by the name of Hen and Chickens Court. If you loiter around for long enough, you're sure to be joined by a tour party. Listen in to their guide, and you will hear the legend of Sweeney Todd, a noted scoundrel whose barber's shop stood next to the courtyard.

You've probably heard the story. Barber Todd would deliver the ultimate close shave, slicing his customer's throat with a razor blade then pulling a lever and sending his man toppling into the basement. His accomplice, Mrs Lovett, would then butcher the corpse and turn it into meat pies, sold to much acclaim from her neighbouring shop.

The name of Sweeney Todd first appeared in serialized form in the penny dreadful *The String of Pearls: A Romance* (1846–47). It is a funny kind of romance by modern understanding, with buckets of gore and a cellar full of body parts. There is a love story in there too, albeit an unusual one. In short: girl loses boy; girl suspects barber had something to do with it; girl cross-dresses to get a job with barber; girl discovers crypt full of cadavers; boy rediscovered as Mrs Lovett's chef-slave; boy reveals pies' ghastly content; Lovett poisoned, Todd captured; girl marries boy and lives happily ever after. Such was the violent melodrama of Victorian penny dreadfuls. The authorship is uncertain, but the tale is generally attributed to James Malcolm Rymer and/or Thomas Peckett Prest, a pair of well-known Victorian hacks.

Whoever wrote the story made the whole thing up. Probably. There is no known record of a barber, or any other individual by the name of Sweeney Todd, living on Fleet Street in the eighteenth or nineteenth centuries. The character was almost certainly cobbled together from various folk tales and criminal reports, a chopped-up composite much like one of Mrs Lovett's pies. Earlier reports of a cannibalistic baker in Paris have been posited as an influence. A stronger candidate can be found in the work of Charles Dickens. One of the characters in *Martin Chuzzlewit* alludes to legends of murderous pastry chefs, hoping that a friend does not 'begin to be afraid that I have strayed into one of those streets where the countrymen are murdered; and that I have been made into meat pies, or some such horrible thing'. *Chuzzlewit* was published two years before *The String of Pearls*. The latter story's supposed authors Rymer and Prest were noted for their parodies of Dickens's novels.

We cannot absolutely rule out a more direct role model for Sweeney Todd. However, nobody has ever produced a press account, or any other piece of printed evidence to back up the Todd story. It is very unlikely that the newspapers would overlook a juicy tale of murder, deception and cannibalism, especially given that the supposed crimes took place within their very midst on Fleet Street.

Non-existence hasn't stymied the brutal barber's popularity. *The String of Pearls* was soon copied, parodied, expanded, embellished, and adapted for stage and then screen. Indeed, a version of the story found its way into a Hoxton theatre while *The String of Pearls* was still being serialized.

The name and the legend live on today, reinforced with every generation. 'The Sweeney' became cockney rhyming slang for 'the Flying Squad', a branch of the Metropolitan Police concerned with heist crime. (The rules of rhyming slang dictate that the part that rhymes – Todd – is dropped from the moniker.) The phrase was subsequently used as the title of a 1970s police drama. Also in that decade, Stephen Sondheim and Hugh Wheeler returned Todd to the London stage with a Tony Award-winning musical version of the barber's nefarious career. Sweeney Todd's star rose again in 2007 with the release of Tim Burton's horror film based on the Sondheim/Wheeler musical. It was very successful, winning two Golden Globes and an Academy Award, and scooping more than $150 million at the box office. It suggests that our appetite for the murderous hairdresser will never be sated.

Jack the Ripper stalked the fog-veiled streets of Whitechapel dressed in top hat and cloak

The Whitechapel murders of 1888 have spawned a whole subgenre of crime literature. New books on the subject are published every year, while the amount of material available online sailed clear past the shores of 'overwhelming' a decade ago. This corpse-laden corpus is riddled with inconsistencies, errors, false assertions and misinterpretations. So much so that my publisher might like to consider commissioning a book called *Everything You Know About Jack The Ripper Is Wrong*. Space (and sanity) does not allow me to dissect this tangled mess in any detail. We shall suffice with a few of the more enduring Ripper myths.

Picture the Ripper in your mind's eye. You no doubt see a cloaked man entirely dressed in black. His face is obscured, perhaps by the shadow from his top hat. He clutches a medical bag in one hand and a bloody knife in the other. The Victorian fog swirls around the villain, and then he is gone into the night.

This popular image of the killer is almost certainly wrong. The East End of the 1880s was chronically impoverished, and populated almost entirely by the labouring classes. Anyone walking around in a top hat and cape would have been conspicuous and thereby ill-suited to stealth.

The impression also contradicts the most credible eyewitness reports. The police interviewed dozens of people who might have seen the killer before or after the foul deeds. All sightings are to some degree circumstantial, and we have no single description that can confidently be ascribed to the killer. One of the best, however, comes from Joseph Lawende, who believed he saw victim Catherine Eddowes walk with a man into Mitre Square, just ten minutes before her body was found there. He described the man as 'of shabby appearance, about 30 years of age and 5 ft 9 in. in height, of fair complexion, having a small fair moustache, and wearing a red neckerchief and a cap with a peak'. Other accounts vary greatly, and may not be reliable, but none suggest a tall hat or cape. Curiously for conspiracy theorists, three witnesses reported an individual wearing a deerstalker hat.

And what of the swirling fog? It is true that Victorian London suffered from frequent pea-soupers – dense fogs caused by the burning of coal in every dwelling and place of business. The obfuscating problem was not continuous, however. Fog would come and go, varying with atmospheric conditions and the number of fires burning across the hearths of London. Four of the five victims were murdered in August and September, when few coal fires would have been lit. No eyewitness statements mention that the murder evenings were foggy, and meteorological records confirm this. The murderer operated on clear nights. No fog.

Because nobody saw any of the crimes in progress, not one of the eyewitness statements can be taken as a reliable description of the Ripper. It is usually presumed that the killer was male, but a female murderer cannot be ruled out. How about two murderers – one to hold the victim, the other to wield the knife? This, too, cannot be dismissed. Ripperologists also disagree on which murders should be attributed to the Ripper. Jack is usually ascribed five killings, but the tally is not certain. One or more of the victims might have been despatched by a different killer, perhaps a copycat or simply another brutal thug walking the streets. Others believe that the Ripper killed more than five times. Whitechapel and its environs were the scene of many other attacks in the years before and after the Ripper. Was his career longer than is normally assumed?

The very name of Jack the Ripper may be an invention of the press. The epithet was first used in the infamous "Dear Boss" letter dated 25 September 1888. Its author taunts the police and press for not getting close to catching him (two of the five canonical murders had been committed at this point). The author promises to clip the ears off his next victim and send them to the police. The epistle is written in red ink (a substitute for the author's bottle of blood, which had gone 'thick like glue'). It is signed 'Yours truly Jack the Ripper ... Don't mind me giving the trade name'.

The letter was at first dismissed as a hoax. The police took more notice a few days later, however, when the body of Catherine Eddowes was discovered with a tear in one ear. The Dear Boss letter was subsequently published in the newspapers in an attempt to trace its author. No credible candidate emerged. Instead, the force was deluged with hoax messages, many carrying the signature of Jack the Ripper.

The Dear Boss letter is now widely thought to be a fake. Its author threatened to remove part of an ear and send it to the police. In fact, Eddowes's ear wound was relatively minor, and no aural package was ever delivered to the constabulary. Nothing else within the missive offers convincing evidence of the killer's authorship. Before long, many came to assume that the letter was another hoax, probably concocted by a journalist to nudge the story's momentum. Several writers confessed to the hoax in the decades afterwards. In any case, the Dear Boss letter gave birth to the Jack the Ripper name. With one flourish of the red pen, the unknown author created the most famous nickname in history.

Of the hundreds of murder letters sent to the police, two others have attracted close attention. The so-called 'Saucy Jack postcard' reached the Central News Agency on 1 October 1888. The author refers to himself as both 'Saucy Jack' and 'Jack the Ripper'. The brief note is written in a similar hand to Dear Boss, and makes reference to that letter, saying 'Had not got time to get ears off for police'. It also mentions a 'double event', alluding to the murders of Eddowes and Liz Stride in the early hours of 30 September. Did the writer have privileged knowledge about crimes that had taken place only the day before? Commentators have argued this point for decades. However, the time stamp on the card is more than 24 hours after the murders – its author could have gleaned details of the slayings from early press reports. It is likely that Dear Boss and Saucy Jack are from the same hand, but there is no clinching reason to attribute either to the murderer himself (or herself, or themselves).

The final key letter was sent to George Lusk of the Whitechapel Vigilance Committee on 16 October 1888. The message was addressed 'From Hell', and written in a distracted style very different to the previous two letters. The author enclosed a gruesome trophy for Mr Lusk: 'I send you half the Kidne I took from one women prasarved it for you tother piece I fried and ate it was very nise.' Subsequent pathological analysis revealed that the kidney was indeed human, and from the left side of the body. This tallied with the mutilations of Catherine Eddowes, whose left kidney had been removed by her killer. The coincidence might seem persuasive. However, details of the coroner's enquiry, including notes on the missing kidney, were widely circulated in the press a few days before the From Hell letter. The authorities soon deemed the episode a gruesome prank, probably by medical students.

In short, none of the three most plausible letters, nor any of supposed eyewitnesses, provides definitive evidence of the killer or killers. We can not say with certainty what the Ripper looked like, how old he was, whether 'he' was indeed male, or even if there was one individual who committed all the crimes. The Whitechapel murders (one of which, Eddowes, took place not in Whitechapel, but the City of London) remain unsolved to this day, despite the sensational revelations of each new Ripper book.

Boris Johnson is the Lord Mayor of London

At the time of writing, Boris Johnson is entering the last few months of his job, having served eight years as Mayor of London. An outsider to the capital might be forgiven for assuming that Johnson had inherited the role most famously occupied by Dick Whittington: Lord Mayor of London. Not so. The *Lord Mayor* presides over only a tiny fraction of the capital, that strange little territory known as the City of London. He or she is elected for just one year to serve as a world ambassador for the Square Mile, and particularly its financial services. The Lord Mayor gets to wear ridiculously opulent robes, ponderous gold chains and other trappings of office. He or she will also ride around (at least once) in a gilded horse-drawn coach, while living and working from a building known as Mansion House.

The *Mayor of London*, by contrast, presides over the whole of Greater London. He or she is responsible for key aspects of city life, including transport, policing and the fire brigade. The Mayor of London boasts no ceremonial robes and – at least in the case of the present incumbent (at the time of writing) – is often seen wobbling around London on a bicycle. His or her office is more prosaically known as City Hall. This bulbous riverside building was dubbed 'the glass testicle' by the first Mayor of London, Ken Livingstone. Mansion House it ain't.

Two mayors might seem confusing, but the waters get still muddier. Every one of London's 32 boroughs also has its own mayor, who steers the borough council. This species of mayor is internally appointed in most cases, although some boroughs (Hackney, Lewisham, Newham, Tower Hamlets) put the vote out to their constituents. All of this means that some Londoners are represented by three mayors. Those who work in the City but live elsewhere can look up to the Lord Mayor, the Mayor of London and their borough mayor.

Subterranean London

London beneath London is a half-glimpsed, mysterious place. Most of us only ever get to see the Tube network, or perhaps a foot or road tunnel, but the capital is also criss-crossed by a bewildering collection of sewers, utility tunnels, air-raid shelters, governmental tunnels and a dozen other flavours of catacomb. It is unsurprising that this netherworld has spawned its own legends and false facts.

Buckingham Palace has its own private tube station

It's the ultimate expression of royal privilege: Her Majesty the Queen has access to her own august tube station beneath Buckingham Palace. In the event of a catastrophic event in the capital, she would simply have to take the royal lift down to the Victoria Line, which runs directly under the palace.

In all honesty, I've never had an invitation to inspect the royal basement and cannot definitively debunk this one. The existence of a private tube stop is almost certainly nonsense, however. While the Victoria Line does pass beneath the palace, the construction of a dedicated entrance would be hard to keep secret from the thousands of contractors who have worked on the line. In any case, the Queen would surely flee by helicopter if the nukes were in the air. It would be much faster, and wouldn't be reliant on the electricity grid's continued operation.

More plausible is some kind of foot tunnel connecting the palace to the governmental tunnels at Westminster. The so-called Q-Whitehall complex of tunnels between key buildings certainly does exist, although its full extent is secret. It would not be beyond the bounds of possibility that a side tunnel might link up with the royal residence, along with St James's Palace and Clarence House. Journalists have independently verified that the subterranean corridors of power extend at least as far as Holborn, so why not to Buck Pal, too? If I ever manage to get down there, I'll let you know.

The basement of the Viaduct Tavern on Newgate Street contains old cells from Newgate Prison

Newgate Prison was, for centuries, the most notorious gaol in the country. Condemned prisoners spent their final days within its walls. Many were executed here. Thousands died from neglect, malnourishment and disease. The prison is long gone, replaced at the turn of the twentieth century by the Old Bailey, but its reputation lingers on.

A surviving fragment of the gaol can apparently be seen at the Viaduct Tavern, across the road on Newgate Street. This Victorian gin palace is worth a visit for many reasons, not least its highly decorative interior and satisfying Fuller's ales. A further attraction can be found to the right of the bar, where a prominent sign points down to 'the cells' and warns that 'Smokers will be incarcerated'. Once below, five small arches do look, superficially, like they might have once served as prison cells. On the other hand, they also look much like any other pub cellar. Yet the literature is unequivocal. Even the authoritative *London Encyclopedia* categorically states that: 'The cellars were once part of Newgate Prison.'

The claim has been called into doubt by other London historians. The pub was constructed in 1869, when Newgate was still very much in use. Would the prison have sacrificed its cells to make way for a beer cellar? Well, possibly. But the evidence stacks up against the claim. For example, chutes often described as 'feeding tubes' for the prisoners are, in reality, nothing more sinister than coal-holes, as still sported by many Victorian buildings. The pub itself no longer goes along with the Newgate line, instead asserting that its 'cells' are from the Giltspur Street Compter, a smaller prison north of Newgate. Alas, the footprint of the building is outside the boundary of the old compter, so this seems unlikely too. While we cannot definitively dismiss claims for prison cells beneath the pub, nobody has yet provided proof to support the story.

A similar claim is made at the Morpeth Arms on the bank of the Thames at Pimlico. The pub reckons that its cellars contain a series of holding cells, used for convicts awaiting transportation. The basement does indeed contain a row of arched chambers, but again this is nothing out of the ordinary for a pub cellar. As with the Holborn case, the pub was built outside the footprint of the prison, so again it seems unlikely that these are old cells.

Scientific analysis of London Underground carriage seats found traces of vomit, semen and human faeces

Given that the London Underground transports one and a quarter billion passengers each year, it is surprisingly rare to find significant litter or mess, a testament to the network's hardworking cleaners. That doesn't stop the repetition of old rumours about the seat covers. To sit down upon a tube train is to park your posterior in an obnoxious mulch of bodily discharge, and there's scientific evidence to prove it, apparently.

According to the accounts commonly found across the Internet, no less an organ than *Science*, one of the world's most respected research journals, ran a story in 2001 that revealed just how unpleasant those pretty seat moquettes really are. According to the report, a team at University College London's Department of Forensics took swabs from a row of seats on the Central Line. Their analysis reads like a witch's brew:

• Four types of hair (human, mouse, rat, dog)
• Seven types of insect (mostly fleas, mostly alive)
• The vomit of at least nine people
• The urine of four people
• Human excrement
• Rodent excrement
• Human semen

Digging down behind the seats, the team discovered further horrors. Just one row of seats yielded the remains of six mice, two large rats and a species of fungus previously unknown to science.

It is a damning indictment of the London Underground. Only, the scientific study is impossible to track down. *Science* journal is well indexed online, and holds no mention of anything approaching such an analysis. UCL does not even have a full forensics department. The report never existed, but its supposed contents spread far and wide by our credulous acceptance that public transport must always be yucky.

This is not to say that the Underground does not have its grime. It seems quite plausible that a sensitive test of a seat cover might find minute traces of sick, for example. It's just that the commonly circulated tale of rats, poo and fleas is a fake. No such research has ever been published.

A number of related studies *have* been done on the Underground, however. In 2013, a team at the London School of Hygiene and Tropical Medicine found that using the London Underground gives no increased risk of catching flu, despite the crushing crowds. The same year, researchers at the University of Bath found that the air in London Underground stations typically contains about twice as many fungal cells as the air in a park. Interestingly, different lines favoured different species, perhaps because of variations in humidity and connectedness to the outside. *Time Out London*, that well-known scholarly journal, provided the most convincing evidence of dirt in 2014. A team of video reporters clobbered Tube seats with a rubber mallet to see how much dust would be kicked up. The answer: lots.

Finally, an icky tangent. Whenever an unpleasant stain does appear on the London Underground, staff use a set of codes to alert cleaning staff without perturbing the public. For example, you might hear an announcement requesting the presence of a cleaner in the main ticket hall to deal with a 'code 3'. Here's what they're talking about:

• Code 1: Blood
• Code 2: Urine/faeces
• Code 3: Vomit
• Code 4: Spillage
• Code 5: Broken glass
• Code 6: Litter
• Code 7: Anything not covered by codes 1–6

This system is remarkable for any number of reasons. Why, for example, does blood have its own code, while urine and faeces are united in rank embrace? Why bother with a code for litter, when no passenger will be distressed by such an announcement? And what in the devil's lunchbox could fall under the remit of code 7? Lymphatic seepage? Synovial fluids? The mind boggles.

Always remember to touch in and touch out

London's transport system depends on an electronic payment technology called Oyster. You can also use contactless debit and credit cards to move around, along with other electronic means. Whichever system you use, posters all over the network will remind you to always 'touch in and touch out' when travelling around. It's not quite as simple as that, however, with numerous exceptions and complications. Time for a bit of verse:

Always touch in and always touch out,
When using your contactless card.
Except on a bus, where you only touch in,
Remember: it isn't that hard.

Always touch in and always touch out,
When seeking to travel by rail.
Except on the tram, down old Croydon way,
Where touch-outs would count as a fail.

Always touch in and always touch out,
But don't touch a thing in the middle.
Except if you travel through some outer zones,
Where pink touch-pads add to the riddle.

Always touch in and always touch out,
Your card works on all transport modes.
Except for the bikes: to hire one of these,
You must dick around with pin codes.

Always touch in and always touch out,
You don't need to wait in a line.
Except on the Clippers, where tickets are king,
You'll need one to ride on the brine.

Always touch in and always touch out,
You'll soon reach your maximum cap.
Except on the Javelin and Thames cable car,
Who'll both give your wallet a slap.

Always touch in and always touch out,
You'll find you can board any train.
Except for the grouchy old Heathrow Express,
Conformity is such a pain.

Always touch in and always touch out,
For Oyster is now here to stay,
Except that we're shifting to contactless cards,
And hipsters all use Apple Pay.

· THEYDON BOIS ·

DEPT

RUISLIP

PLAISTOW

HOMERTON

MARYL

LEICESTER SQUARE

THE MALL SW1

PLAISTO

HOLBORN EC1

HO

· THEYDON BOIS ·

LEICE

London language

NE

YDON BOIS

RUISLIP

RTON

Place names are protean in a city as old as this. 'London' itself is only the most recent spelling for our town. If we could travel back through time we would find ourselves in Lundenburh (ninth–eleventh centuries), Lundenwic (seventh–ninth centuries), Augusta (fourth century), or Londinium and its variants (first–fourth centuries). Some linguists have suggested the area might have been known as Plowonida in Celtic times.

This ever-changing gazetteer spawns all manner of errors, myths, odd pronunciations and false etymologies. Such misconceptions are explored in this chapter. We start with a few notes on different areas of London, and then move on to a few phrases said to originate in the city's past.

SQUARE

DEPTFORD

D

Elephant and Castle is named after La Infanta de Castilla

It's fair to say that Elephant and Castle is among the capital's more unusual place names. Peculiarity breeds speculation, and the busy road junction and area in south London has attracted many fanciful etymologies. Chief among them is the theory that Elephant and Castle takes its name from a Spanish princess.

'Infanta de Castilla' is the traditional title given to certain Spanish princesses. The English royal family has often married into Iberian stock. Most prominent was Eleanor of Castile (1240–1290), the queen of Edward I – we met her earlier in the discussion about the centre of London. To have a notorious gyratory system named after you might be a great honour, but it is not one that Eleanor can boast. She died 300 years before the infanta title came into use. Too early, also, was Catherine of Aragon, one of the many wives of Henry VIII. Another candidate might be Maria Anna of Spain, youngest daughter of Philip III. This one-time squeeze of Charles I did carry the title of infanta, but she never married Charles and had no connection with Castile. In any case, the Newington area around the Elephant has little history with royalty of any stripe.

Could the area be named after a genuine elephant? London has had a surprisingly long association with pachyderms. Mammoth skeletons have been found beneath Trafalgar Square, Canary Wharf and other locations. The first elephant visited the area during the Roman invasion around AD 40. The historian Polyaenus records how 'Caesar had one large elephant, which was equipped with armour and carried archers and slingers in its tower. When this unknown creature entered the river, the Britons and their horses fled and the

Roman army crossed over.' More than a millennium would pass before the next trunk was seen in Britain. This came courtesy of Louis IX of France, who gifted a beast to Henry III in 1255. The elephant was kept in the Tower of London. According to chronicler Matthew Paris, it did not last long, and supposedly died from a 'surfeit of wine' just two years later. So far as we can know, none of these beasts troubled the Newington area.

The busy junction is almost certainly named after an Elephant and Castle coaching inn, which was documented as far back as 1735. Shakespeare, too, was perhaps referring to the hostelry in *Twelfth Night*, where he writes: 'In the south suburbs, at the Elephant, is best to lodge.' He was speaking of Illyria, but may have been namechecking a London inn that his audience would know.

The symbol of a castellated pachyderm is an ancient one, a stylized depiction of the kind of set-up our friend Polyaenus was describing above. It is also prominent in the coat of arms of the Worshipful Company of Cutlers (ivory was used for knife handles), and herein may lie the true etymology of Elephant and Castle. It is possible that a cutler's workshop became an inn, which took the sign of the cutlers in deference to the building's former use. Nobody knows for sure. We're left with an elephant-sized hole for rival theorists to exploit.

We need to protect London's traditional place names, like Fitzrovia

Property developers and business groups are ruining London, dicking about with long-established place names and coining monstrosities. The most pernicious is 'Midtown', conjured up in the noughties as a catch-all term for Bloomsbury, St Giles and Holborn. The commonest form of rebranding is to dub an area a 'quarter'. Most things in life have four quarters. Not London. We had over 20 the last time I counted, from the Ram Quarter in Wandsworth to the Knowledge Quarter in King's Cross. And then there is the 'village', with such delights as Portman Village in the west and East Village in the Olympic Park. It's easy to rail against these paint-by-committee decisions, but the truth is that the neighbourhoods of London have long been slippery of name.

Who now remembers the settlement of Horsleydown in Bermondsey, or Garratt in Wandsworth? What happened to Agar Town near Camden? In days of yore, New Cross was known as Hatcham and King's Cross as Battle Bridge. Names change all the time. The process may have accelerated, but it has always been with us: Londinium, Lundenwic, Lundenburh, London.

Fitzrovia offers another case in point. Every now and then, some wag comes along and suggests the district be redubbed 'Noho', as a northern corollary to Soho. 'This is not Manhattan', scream the traditionalists, thinking of New York City, which has both a SoHo and a Noho. 'We must protect Fitzrovia!'

All well and good, but the current name is not as established as many think. Until the 1950s, the area was normally bundled in as part of Soho. The phrase 'Fitzrovia' was not in polite use at all before the Second World War. Its first occurrence in print was in a 1940 gossip column in the *Daily Express*. *The Times* wouldn't touch the word until 1958, and even then felt the need to distance itself from such vulgarity by smothering 'Fitzrovia' in quotation marks. As late as 1963, that same newspaper would describe the area as 'what the tavern Bohemians romantically call Fitzrovia and realists might describe as the shabby side of Tottenham Court Road'.

The term derives from the Fitzroy family, historic owners of the land. They begat Fitzroy Square, Fitzroy Street and, in the early twentieth century, the Fitzroy Tavern. 'Fitzrovia' as an area name only began to creep in during the 1930s, when the tavern became the spiritual home of a thirsty set of wordsmiths centring on Julian MacLaren-Ross and Dylan Thomas. It did not gain popular currency until a couple of decades later.

It may not have antiquity on its side, but 'Fitzrovia' is, to many, a better neologism than 'Noho'. The latter term has surfaced a number of times over the decades, most recently as the proposed name (Noho Square) of a new development on the site of Middlesex Hospital. The prospect of a top-down imposed name with American overtone caused much uproar and the plans (and name) were changed. Good not-so-old 'Fitzrovia' remains the universal term for the area. For now.

Are you pronouncing it wrongly?

Most London place names are very old. Former villages like Kennington, Wembley, Brixton, Dagenham and Tottenham are named after Anglo-Saxon chieftains, landowners or landmarks. Some are older still. If the word 'Penge' makes you chuckle, it's perhaps because its name is pre-Roman and therefore unusually ancient. It sounds peculiar to the ear.

London's place names have evolved over centuries, sometimes retaining archaic pronunciations while evolving into a modern spelling. This throws up a gazetteer of fricative anomalies and silent consonants, which are the bane of every lost tourist, and many a local too. Have you ever struggled with 'Plaistow' or 'Theydon Bois'? Here's a guide to the most common stumbling blocks.

Chiswick, Greenwich, Southwark, Woolwich: Notice how all these places are close to the Thames? It's no coincidence. The wark/wich ending suggests an Anglo-Saxon landing place. In such cases, just forget about the 'w'. 'Chiz-ick', for example. Aldwych is an anomaly, which should probably drop its 'w', but refuses – perhaps because 'Ald-itch' sounds like a longstanding skin complaint. In addition, some denizens of Greenwich and Woolwich insist on giving their towns an 'idge' ending. To sound local, go for 'Grin-idge' or 'Wool-idge'.

Deptford: This is 'Det-ford' ... don't pronounce the 'p', just as you wouldn't enunciate the 'b' in debt.

Dulwich: Make this a 'Dull-itch'. Despite its name, Dulwich is not on the river like Woolwich and Greenwich, but probably derives its suffix from the Anglo-Saxon *wihs*, meaning 'damp meadow' (where dill grows).

Leicester Square: All Brits should know that this is pronounced 'Less-ter', but the tricky sequence of vowels is a famous impediment for visitors.

Hainault: The Central Line stop favours the English pronunciation of 'Hay-nolt', rather than the Gallic 'Ay-no' one might expect.

Holborn: The trick here is to use as few letters as possible – 'O'b'n' rather than 'Hole-born'. Or, pronounce it 'Midtown' and wait for the angry retorts.

The Mall: American visitors might be expecting a shopping centre, but the royal road is pronounced with a short 'a', to rhyme with 'pal', not 'Paul'. As it happens, the name was imported from the neighbouring Pall Mall (definitely not pronounced 'Paul Maul'), which itself got its name from a croquet-like game called Pell Mell.

Marylebone: As with 'Holborn', jettison as many letters as you can get away with. 'Mar'l'bun' is a good start.

Plaistow: A regularly mispronounced name. Say 'Plaaaahstow', not 'Play-stow'.

Ruislip: This one's 'Ry-slip'.

Strand: Nobody has a problem with the pronunciation, but there is some confusion on whether it should be 'Strand' or 'the Strand'. Purists maintain that the road name does not contain a 'the', so it should be omitted in careful writing – much as we wouldn't say 'the Holborn' or 'the Whitehall' to refer to those streets. This is debatable. The oldest maps show the street labelled as 'the Stronde' or 'the Strand' ('strand' is a synonym for 'shore' or 'beach', a geographical reference to the Thames). Dropping the 'the' was a Victorian intervention, but it is now perpetuated in the street signs. In any case, no Londoner, now or then, would say 'Let's all go down Strand'.

Streatham: 'Stret-um'. However, such is the pace of gentrification that an increasing contingent sardonically call the area 'Saint Reatham'.

Theydon Bois: The consensus seems to be 'Theydon Boyce' (or 'Boyz'), rather than the Frenchified 'Theydon Bwahh'.

Spelling and punctuation

You might be pronouncing London's place names correctly, but are you getting the punctuation wrong? Apostrophes, in particular, can be a fiendishly complicated business when it comes to London locations.

King's Cross provides a particularly revealing example. The place name now sports a prominent apostrophe in the A–Z, on the Tube map and on mainline station signage. All three omitted the mark for the first half of the twentieth century, however. Early newspaper reports even included a hyphen, giving us Kings-Cross and King's-Cross.

The apostrophe is applied whimsically by the local authority (Camden Council) and the Mayor's office; sometimes it is present, sometimes absent. The King's Cross Central development uses a bright red apostrophe in emphatic support of the punctuation. The contrarian *Guardian* has its headquarters in the nearby Kings Place, while insisting on King's Cross in its style guide. It seems that the apostrophe falls in and out of fashion. There is no official stance on the name. Or, if there is, no one sticks to it.

It could be argued, persuasively, that the mark is warranted. The area takes its name from a long-vanished memorial dedicated to George IV. A possessive apostrophe to indicate the cross of the king therefore makes sense. It is, however, somewhat redundant. Apostrophes are useful tools in written prose, but are less important to place names. No one reads 'Kings Cross' and assumes that multiple monarchs must be crossing the street. It's a label and nothing more. If we can get over that hurdle, an unapostrophized name looks cleaner and works better with modern technologies such as predictive text, search engines and website URLs.

Other anomalies abound. Earl's Court usually flaunts an apostrophe, yet the neighbouring Barons Court is barren of punctuation. Elsewhere on the Tube map, Queen's Park, Regent's Park, Shepherd's Bush, St John's Wood and, of course, St Paul's all take the supplementary character. Would we really lose anything if such stations joined the likes of Golders Green, Colliers Wood and Parsons Green in eschewing the mark? And then there's the case of King's Road. The A–Z map gives it an apostrophe at the western end, but not at the eastern. Road signs along this route also vary. This is before we get into arguments about whether it should be King's Road or *the* King's Road.

In short, it's all a big mess. Which is as it should be, because everybody loves arguing about punctuation and grammar. Long live the equivocal apostrophe.

That's not my name

Many a visitor has struggled to find Petticoat Lane. The road is noted for its market, where inexpensive clothes, fabrics and trinkets can be purchased on any Sunday. Like a magical location from *Harry Potter*, however, you won't find Petticoat Lane on the map. The road changed its name to 'Middlesex Street' two centuries ago – partly to reflect the Middlesex boundary with the City of London, and partly because decision makers of the time thought that 'Middlesex Street' was more euphonious than 'Petticoat Lane'. The rebranding didn't help. A newspaper commentator of 1845 reckoned, 'It is the same filthy, badly-paved street as it ever was, and its equal for dirt, crime and immorality is scarcely to be found in England ... Although Middlesex Street is painted on the walls on each side of the lane, Petticoat-lane it is still called and is likely ever to be so.' That writer's prediction still holds true 170 years later – the street and its environs are still regularly referred to as 'Petticoat Lane'.

The example shows the power of names. The city authorities might dictate the street signs, but popular sentiment often carries a lingering influence. London itself is still known as 'the Big Smoke', long after the coal fires were extinguished.

The city's skyscrapers are particularly prone to neologism. Most have an official, boring street address, but are swiftly given nicknames, affectionate or otherwise. 'The Gherkin', for example, is 'wrong' as far as its owners are concerned. They refer to the building as '30 St Mary Axe'; nobody else does, other than their PR firm.

Official names will now often include a corporate sponsor. When the banking giant Santander set aside £43.75 million to secure sponsor's rights for the city's cycle hire scheme, it paid for the privilege of getting its name all over the bikes. Hence, we now pedal around on Santander Cycles. Londoners, however, have a healthy scepticism towards marketeering. The cycles are called 'Boris Bikes'

Nickname(s)	Correct name	Previous name(s)
Big Ben	Elizabeth Tower	The Clock Tower, St Stephen's Tower (erroneously)
Boris Bikes	Santander Cycles	Barclays Cycle Hire
Boris Bus	New Routemaster	New Bus For London
The Can of Ham*	60–70 St Mary Axe	
The Cheese Grater	The Leadenhall Building	
The Dangleway**, the cable car	Emirates Air Line	
The Dome	The O2	Millennium Dome
The Drain	Waterloo and City Line	Waterloo and City Railway
The Glass Testicle***	City Hall	
Millennium Wheel	Coca-Cola London Eye	British Airways London Eye
Petticoat Lane	Middlesex Street	Petticoat Lane
The Tangled Earphones, The Squiggle, The Eyesore, Mittal Orbit, The Orbit Tower	The ArcelorMittal Orbit	
The Walkie-Talkie	20 Fenchurch Street	
The Wobbly Bridge	London Millennium Footbridge	

after the Mayor, by just about everyone (even though his predecessor, Ken Livingstone, set the scheme in motion).

With their distaste for top-down authority, Londoners have coined many other nicknames for the buildings and services of their city. Sobriquets like 'Gherkin' and 'Cheese Grater' may be officially 'wrong', but they might also be considered democratically virtuous. Wouldn't you rather live in a city where the landmarks are named by popular consent, rather than imposed by politicians and capitalists?

Nevertheless, in this book's spirit of nitpicking, we need to untangle this confusion of appellations. On the previous page is a list of London locations and services you might be familiar with. All these nicknames are officially 'wrong'; you'll find the 'correct' name alongside, with any earlier names.

---

*FOOTNOTE: A proposed building, of self-explanatory shape, yet to begin construction in the City.
**FOOTNOTE: Coined by blogger Diamond Geezer, and gaining popular currency.
***FOOTNOTE: A term coined by Ken Livingstone for his future headquarters as Mayor.

The phrase 'on the wagon' has its origins in London executions

Those who abstain from alcohol, having previously enjoyed a tipple, are said to be 'on the wagon'. It's a curious phrase, with little obvious connection to booze. The term is often attributed to the days when criminals would make their final journey from Newgate gaol to the gallows at Tyburn (modern-day Marble Arch) on the back of a wagon. The route passed by many taverns, at which the condemned might be allowed a final stiff drink to ease their torment. Having partaken, the luckless individual would resume his or her last journey 'on the wagon'.

However, the phrase seems to have been coined in the early twentieth century, on another continent and long after the time of public executions. The US temperance movement was in full swing, with many Americans taking water rather than alcohol. Such abstainers would declare themselves 'on the water cart', in a jokey reference to the machinery used to hose down dusty roads. This soon migrated to 'on the water wagon'. With familiarity, this was shortened to 'on the wagon', the phrase we still use today. The term was common enough by 1908 to appear in a list of 'funny idioms' used by Americans. In an Australian newspaper article of that year, 'riding on the water wagon' is joined by other peculiar terms, now familiar, such as 'full of hot air', 'deliver the goods' and a 'steady' partner.

The phrase 'one for the road' is part of the same linguistic cocktail. It is said that the condemned prisoners would stop at a hostelry on the way to Tyburn gallows, and enjoy a final alcoholic drink 'for the road'. The origins of this term are a little more fuzzy, but there is no reason to assume it was the toast of the doomed. Many of us have felt the urge to prolong a drinking session with good friends or new acquaintances. 'One for the road?' hardly needs an origin story – we've all craved that final drink before hitting the streets, and it might have been coined at any time by anybody. The earliest reference I can find is from a women's newspaper column in November 1937. Its context, and similar occurrences in the late 1930s, suggest that the phrase – worryingly – came into common use during the growth of motoring.

In any case, the idea that prisoners frequently stopped for a drink en route to the gallows is fanciful. Any execution came with the danger of mob agitation, or even rescue attempts. Prisoners would have been conveyed to the gallows with as little complication as possible. Stopping off at a roadside tavern would have presented numerous security headaches, and there are few reliable sources that allude to the practice. Nevertheless, several London pubs claim the dubious honour of lubricating the throats of the condemned. The Swan on Bayswater Road goes as far as to say that 'on the wagon' and 'one for the road' were first coined within its walls. It's a particularly bold assertion, given that prisoners coming from Newgate would have to go half a mile beyond Tyburn to reach the pub.

The phrase 'at sixes and sevens' was invented by London livery companies in a dispute over precedence

To be at sixes and sevens is to be in contretemps; to have an ongoing dispute with another party. Etymologists offer numerous explanations of where the phrase comes from. One of the most popular concerns the City of London livery companies. A peculiarity of this guild system is that all livery companies place themselves somewhere in a pecking order based on a combination of age and historic wealth. The Worshipful Company of Mercers holds the top spot by virtue of its great antiquity – it got a royal charter in 1394, but existed long before. The Worshipful Company of Art Scholars props up the list in 104th place. It only came into existence in 2014.*

The order of precedence hits a snag with the Skinners and Merchant Taylors. Both companies bagged a royal charter in the same year, 1327, leading to a dispute: who should be sixth and who should be seventh? The bickering was ended in 1484 by the Lord Mayor, Robert Billesdon (or Billesden if you're a Merchant Taylor – the two companies insist on different spellings). He decreed that the squabbling parties would henceforth swap priority annually. Skinners would be sixth one year, Merchant Taylors the next. The tradition continues today, only interrupted if a member of either company becomes Lord Mayor.

So is this the origin of the phrase 'at sixes and sevens'? It seems convincing, and many livery companies perpetuate the story on their websites and tours. But one inconvenient truth, in the mischievous shape of Geoffrey Chaucer, sullies the legend. His *Troilus and Criseyde* contains the lines: 'Lat nat this wrecched wo thyn herte gnawe, But manly sette the world on six and sevene.' Those words were written around 1385, a century before the Billesdon/Billesden declaration.

Chaucer is talking about a dice game, in which throwing a six or seven comes with some jeopardy. Other references to the numbers occur throughout the fourteenth and fifteenth centuries – it was clearly a well-known phrase. That said, we cannot entirely expunge the livery companies from the etymological record. The argument of precedence may have been raging decades before the Lord Mayor solved it. His solution, creating an alternation for sixth and seventh place, might have reinforced the existing phrase, adding new context and ensuring its survival. Think of Rachmaninoff's Piano Concerto No. 2. The composition was popular 45 years before *Brief Encounter*, but that film gave the soul-stirring orchestration a new lease of life, boosting the music's popularity and endurance. So might have happened with our sixes and sevens – an old phrase given a new fillip by warring liverymen. File this one under 'Nobody knows for sure'.

---

*FOOTNOTE: And therein lies a digression. A common myth is that all livery companies are venerable, medieval throwbacks. Not so. Almost a third came into existence over the past century. As well as the Art Scholars, these include such organizations as the Worshipful Company of Information Technologists and the Worshipful Company of Water Conservators. I'm hoping to create the Worshipful Company of Nitpickers, should this book be successful.

Nylon was discovered by teams working in New York and London, hence it was called NYLon

Scientific research is the most international of pursuits, so this oft-repeated etymology certainly has a ring of veracity. Sadly, the truth is more prosaic. The first nylon was synthesized by Wallace Carothers in 1935. His team was based at DuPont Experimental Station in Delaware, with no obvious connection to either New York or London. The polymer was known as Fiber 66 during the experimental phase, and was first marketed as nylon in 1938. Production did not begin in the UK until 1941, and then in Coventry, not in London.

DuPont has issued two contradictory origin stories for the name of its product. A 1940 statement explains that the suffix comes from the generic ending for fibres such as cotton and rayon, while the prefix 'nyl' is arbitrary. A 1978 publication instead suggests the name was derived from 'no-run' – as in 'You won't be able to ladder these'. Clearly delusive, 'no-run' became 'nylon' and a phenomenon was born. Either way, London played no part in its development. New York did, however, see an early wave of nylon fever when a fabric made from the fibres was first demonstrated to the public during the 1939 World's Fair.

A miscellany of misnomers and false etymologies

Abbey Road: A station on the Docklands Light Railway that is indeed near a former abbey, but many miles from the Abbey Road of Beatles fame. So many fans make the mistaken pilgrimage that the station now displays a poster with directions to the north London recording studios.

Bond Street: The Central and Jubilee Line station serves a road that does not exist. You'll find a New Bond Street and an Old Bond Street on the map, but not plain Bond Street.

Boris Johnson: Universally known as 'Boris', the mop-headed London MP and second Mayor of London trades under one of his middle names. To give him his full dues, call him Alexander Boris de Pfeffel Johnson. The peculiar 'de Pfeffel' is a hand-me-down name from BoJo's aristocratic German ancestors.

Cannon Street: Nothing to do with military cannon, nor religious canons. Rather, it is a truncation of the medieval Candelwrichstrete – the area of town dominated by candle makers.

Charing Cross Hospital: Lurks five miles from Charing Cross, in the Hammersmith-Fulham borders. The hospital moved away from Charing Cross in 1973, but kept the name. As though to preserve some credibility to its title, the main hospital building has a cross-shaped plan.

Circle Line: London's yellow Tube line never was a circle. On older Underground maps it looked more like a bottle lying on its side. If drawn to accurate geography, the line was even more irregular, resembling a lethargic monk reclining on the Thames. Nowadays, the Circle isn't even a topological hoop. In 2009, the line was extended round on to Hammersmith and City tracks, taking it farther west and south. It might more accurately be termed the Spiral Line.

BOTTLE   LETHARGIC MONK   SPIRAL LINE
RECLINING ON THE THAMES   (SINCE 2009)

Clapham Junction: Despite its name, this busy railway station is not in Clapham. It's not even in the same borough as Clapham. It's actually located in Battersea, in the Borough of Wandsworth, whereas Clapham proper is in Lambeth. Battersea locals get all wound up if you make this mistake, so be sure to do so at any opportunity.

Clerkenwell Green: Can you spot the grass? Me neither. Clerkenwell Green has lacked a green for centuries. Even Charles Dickens noted the absurdity of this name in his 1837 novel *Oliver Twist*: 'not far from the open square in Clerkenwell, which is yet called, by some strange perversion of terms, "The Green"'.

Constitution Hill: This stately road runs to the north of Buckingham Palace. Its proximity to the corridors of power leads to a ready association with political constitutions. However, most sources, including the Royal Parks authority, agree that it takes its name from the 'constitutional' walks enjoyed along the route by nobility and royalty in former centuries. To compound the confusion, Constitution Hill is not noticeably a hill.

Crystal Palace dinosaurs: The life-sized models in Crystal Palace Park were created in 1852, when our knowledge of prehistoric animals was much more sketchy than it is today. Consequently, several of the beasts are badly proportioned or anatomically naive. The real 'wrongness' here, though, is to assume that they are all dinosaurs. Actually, only a very small number fit the bill. Of the 29 animals depicted in the park, only four are true dinosaurs, and 25 are from other animal groups such as early mammals, pterosaurs, ichthyosaurs and crocodilians. Try telling that to your five-year-old, though.

Finsbury Park: A park (and tube station) some three miles north of the fomer borough of Finsbury, for whose residents it was created. More importantly, if you say Finsbury park backwards you get a Krapy Rubsnif.

Jubilee Line: This tube line opened in 1979, two years after the Queen's Silver Jubilee. They got the colour right, though.

Kentish Town: It has no connections to Kent. The name is thought to derive from Ken-ditch, a reference to the River Fleet, which passes through the area. The upper reaches of this river were once known as the Ken or Caen, from where we also get the name of Kenwood House on Hampstead Heath.

London Overground: The network of orange lines on the Tube map represents the London Overground. The suburban rail network was launched by Transport for London in 2007, often reusing existing rail lines. Although most of it is indeed overground, it takes a notable subterranean dip through the Thames Tunnel between Wapping and Rotherhithe. At Whitechapel station, something ludicrous happens: the London Overground passes underneath the London Underground. It should also be noted that the London Overground is not entirely confined to the capital. It leaves London in two places to reach Watford and Cheshunt.

London Underground: As above, both moieties of this phrase are partially misleading. While most of the network is inside London, 14 stations are located in the Home Counties. In fact, five of them are beyond the M25 (Amersham, Chalfont and Latimer, Chesham, Chorleywood, and Epping). Meanwhile, the majority of the Underground (55 per cent) is above ground. The Victoria Line and Waterloo and City lines are the only ones entirely underground.

Mansion House Underground station: This is actually the third-closest station to Mansion House. Bank and Cannon Street stations are nearer, and Monument runs things pretty close.

Mount Pleasant: Known chiefly for its large sorting office, Mount Pleasant near Clerkenwell is neither much of a mount, nor particularly pleasant – although decidedly more so than in former centuries, when the land was inhabited by the notorious Coldbath Fields Prison and the foetid River Fleet.

Teddington: Corruption of 'Tide's End Town'. This would seem a plausible derivation. After all, Teddington is usually considered the point upriver where the Thames ceases to feel the influence of the tides. The etymology was given added weight by Rudyard Kipling, who cites it in his poem 'The River's Tale'. The dull truth is that Teddington, like many other places, got its name from a medieval chieftain or landowner, and was first recorded as Totyngton.

Twickenham: So named because it's betwixt Wick and Ham. It's a neat theory, utterly ruined by geography. Twickenham is north of the villages of Hampton Wick and Ham, not between them. The name probably derives from a local landowner called Twicca. It was first recorded in AD 704 as 'Tuicanhom'.

Popular culture

London has been at the centre of almost all
cultural forms for many centuries, and so has spawned
a heap of mistruths.

Sherlock Holmes was fond of saying 'Elementary, my dear Watson'

Much as Captain Kirk never said 'Beam me up Scotty', Sherlock Holmes never uttered the oft-imitated line, 'Elementary, my dear Watson.' Not, at least, in the 60 canonical stories written by Arthur Conan Doyle. The author uses the word 'elementary' on eight occasions and the phrase 'my dear Watson' some 83 times, but the two are never combined.

The line's genesis is unclear. It may have had its origins in William Gillette's stage adaptation, *Sherlock Holmes: A Drama in Four Acts*, which debuted in New York City in 1899. Gillette was the first to bring the detective to the stage with Conan Doyle's blessing and, indeed, Doyle had a hand in the script. The published version has Holmes saying, 'Elementary, my dear fellow.' It's possible but unverifiable that Gillette altered this to 'Watson' on stage. Further adaptations employed the line, and it gradually became Sherlockian vernacular. By the 1920s, the phrase had become a cliché for the detective.

Gillette was responsible for another Holmesian trope. His 1899 play introduced the curving pipe, whereas Doyle and his illustrator Sidney Paget had furnished the detective with a simpler, straighter smoke. Paget, meanwhile, first gave Holmes his deerstalker hat, a piece of headgear never mentioned in the prose.

The 'swinging sixties' were a time of free love, hedonism and high fashion for Londoners

Few things in life are as romanticized as the 'swinging sixties'. It's easy to imagine everybody going around in the latest fashions, with flowers in their hair and enjoying a lifestyle of sex and drugs and rock and roll. This was the era of miniskirts, the Fab Four, the summer of love and ready contraception. When international magazine *Time* ran its 1966 issue devoted to 'London: the Swinging City', all the world swallowed the line that this was the capital of cool. It is a notion still imprinted on our collective memories today, to the point where it has been mercilessly parodied by the likes of the Rutles and the *Austin Powers* films.

In reality, few people had the opportunity to indulge in the hedonism often portrayed in films and newsreels. The 1960s was a decade characterized by economic woes, a crippling shortage of housing, and a lingering conservatism that still governed the habits of many, both young and old. 'The "swinging sixties" did not swing in Lambeth', wrote John Major in his autobiography. Lest the former prime minister does not seem a hip enough example, even Paul Weller admitted that the decade didn't swing for him. Quite the opposite: 'The only reason we eventually had a bathroom was 'cos my old man knocked a f**king hole through the wall in the kitchen and built one', he told one journalist. Weller had it easy. London's growing Afro-Caribbean population found housing particularly difficult to come by, with continued discrimination from landlords.

Only a small, middle-class fraction of London's population could afford to (or cared to) shop on Carnaby Street or spend all day parading down the King's Road. Despite all the psychedelic songs and videos of that era, only around 5 per cent of young adults are thought to have experimented with illegal drugs. Today, as much as a third of the population have done so.

It's true that there had been a significant rise in spending power and disposable income. Old taboos were increasingly challenged. London did become a world centre for fashion, music and film. And yet this was only a beginning, a wellspring. Those who led the way were a fashionable minority. Most people who were there *can* remember the 1960s, though not always as a time of freewheeling, liberal abandon.

Jimi Hendrix released a pair of parakeets from his Carnaby Street flat in the 1960s: now there are thousands of them

The rose-ringed parakeet is steadily supplanting the pigeon and the sparrow as the avian symbol of London. The bright green birds have been spotted in all 32 boroughs, plus the City of London. You'll find them in particularly large flocks in areas such as Richmond Park and Bushy Park to the south-west, and farther out into Surrey. How did the birds, which are native to the Himalayas, come to settle in London?

Theories abound. One suitably colourful myth places their origin on Carnaby Street in the swinging sixties, when guitar legend Jimi Hendrix supposedly released a pair into the wild. It seems unlikely, however, that a population now numbering in the tens of thousands could originate from just two birds. I recently had the opportunity to quiz Kathy Etchingham, Hendrix's girlfriend during his time in London, about the story. She confirmed it was an urban myth, adding that she'd only recently heard it for the first time.

Another dubious explanation puts the pioneer flock as escapees from the set of *The African Queen*, partly filmed at Isleworth Studios. This origin also seems improbable. The parakeet population only really began to boom in the 1990s, 40 years after Hepburn and Bogart's wartime caper.

Perhaps the most convincing theory is that the birds were released from private aviaries during the Great Storm of 1987. The date would fit, and the widespread devastation could have freed enough birds to form a breeding population. Sadly, we're never likely to know for sure, although a genetic analysis could reveal how interrelated the birds are, thus giving us some idea how many escapee birds founded the now-booming population.

Aphex Twin lives in the strange glass and metal structure on the Elephant and Castle roundabout

Bringing this musical section more up to date is this recent urban legend of Aphex Twin, the noted composer of electronic music. Mr Twin, real name Richard David James, once joked that he was about to exchange contracts on the futuristic grey box that adorns the centre of the Elephant and Castle roundabout. Its sleek, silvery lines certainly look like they might belong to a recording studio. Alas, the claim was a fib. Aphex Twin *was* an Elephant resident for several years, but he did not own or live in the silver box. The stainless-steel structure is an electricity substation connected to the Northern Line. It also doubles as a memorial to Michael Faraday, the electrical pioneer whose formative years were spent in the area.

Elephant and Castle seems to be something of a lightning rod for mythology. We've looked elsewhere at the apocryphal origins of the place name. The Elephant was also invoked by Virginia Woolf in *A Room of One's Own*. The author imagines a fictional sister of Shakespeare buried beneath the bus queues of the area, much as Boudicca has been associated with the platforms of King's Cross station.

Bob Holness played the saxophone solo on 'Baker Street'

This enduring myth falls into the 'so bizarre it has to be true' category. Sadly, it's not. Bob Holness was the host of a popular 1980s quiz show, *Blockbusters*. An urban myth got around that he played the saxophone sequence on Gerry Rafferty's 1978 hit 'Baker Street', surely the most recognizable sax riff of all time. The myth does a disservice to session player Raphael Ravenscroft, who was the real lungs behind the solo. The Scotsman was reportedly paid just £27.50 for the work, and the cheque bounced.

Holness, it transpires, was unable to play a note on the saxophone. So where did the legend come from? There are rival claimants. DJ Stuart Maconie has put his name to the unlikely piece of trivia. He claims to have made it up in 1990 for a 'believe it or not' column in the *NME* music newspaper. Another DJ, Tommy Boyd, also seeks the glory. He says that the idea of associating the wholesome Holness with a raunchy sax solo came to him while concocting a quiz for LBC radio, years before Maconie made the fib. Ravenscroft himself is a candidate. At the time of Bob Holness's death in 2012, the saxophonist told the BBC that he'd made the fact up 'because I used to be asked 20 or 30 times if I was the person who did it, so to a foreign journalist I said it was Bob Holness, because I had been working with him on a Robinson's advert. It was just a bit of fun'.

Who knows? What *is* true is that Bob Holness was one of the first people to play James Bond. He starred in a 1957 dramatization of *Moonraker* on South African radio.

Mama Cass choked to death on a ham sandwich in London

'California Dreamin' singer Cass Elliot did indeed die in London, but not from choking on a sandwich. In July 1974, Elliot was in town for a two-week series of solo concerts at the London Palladium. She was staying in a Mayfair apartment hired from fellow singer-songwriter Harry Nilsson. After playing the final concert in the series, she passed away in the apartment aged just 32. An autopsy found that she had died of a heart attack, with no evidence of food in the windpipe. It seems that a police officer had made the mistake of speculating on the cause of death in front of the media. Looking for quick answers, the press leapt upon the fact that a half-eaten sandwich had been found in the room. The flat, at 9 Curzon Place, would hit notoriety again four years later. In a bizarre coincidence, the Who drummer, Keith Moon, died of a drug overdose in the same apartment. He was also aged 32.

Mick Jagger and Keith Richards founded the Rolling Stones after randomly meeting on Dartford station

The windswept platforms of Dartford station, just outside London, are hardly the most glamorous fountainhead for one of the great rock and roll partnerships. But it was here, in 1961, that Mick Jagger got chatting to Keith Richards. The pair were heading into London, Richards clutching his electric guitar, Jagger with a cache of LPs. They had attended the same primary school, but had since lost touch. Their musical accoutrements acted as an ice-breaker on the station, and the subsequent train journey into London marked their first meaningful conversation.

In February 2015, a plaque was unveiled on the station to mark the momentous occasion: 'Mick Jagger and Keith Richards met on Platform 2 on 17 October 1961 and went on to form the Rolling Stones – one of the most successful rock bands of all time.'

Not everyone was impressed. Fellow Stone Bill Wyman described the plaque as 'disgusting'. Why? Dartford Borough Council had made a common error – that Jagger and Richards founded the band – and enshrined it as history on the station platform. It would be more accurate to apportion that honour to

Brian Jones. It was he who placed an advert for bandmates in the music press, and he who chose the name of the Rolling Stones. Jagger and Richards joined early, but were not the founders. The council later acknowledged its error, and a replacement plaque has now been commissioned.

Mick & Co's great rivals, The Beatles, are the subject of London's most famous rock and roll myth, though one so patently false that it doesn't deserve to be mythbusted under its own heading. I speak, of course, about the 'Paul is dead' legend which first gained currency in 1969, and remains well known today. Adherents believe that Paul McCartney died in a car accident in 1966, only to be replaced with a lookalike. The Fab Three Plus Imposter then seeded subsequent releases with hints at Paul's demise. The most famous is the cover of Abbey Road, which depicts the quartet on a zebra crossing outside their studios in north London. According to conspiracy theorists, John Lennon is dressed in white to symbolise a heavenly figure; Ringo, all in black, is the undertaker; George is a gravedigger in jeans and shirt; which makes Paul the corpse, suitably barefoot and out of step with his bandmates.

Plaques that got it wrong

It is no wonder that myths and fabrications about London's history abound. Sometimes even the authorities can't get their information right. We've seen already how Brian Jones was slighted by Dartford Council when he was replaced by Mick and Keith as founder of the Rolling Stones. A surprising number of other plaques spread misinformation.

Wrong bomb

Take, for example, the London Borough of Hackney plaque at the former Nevil Arms public house on Osterley Road. This records the first bomb dropped on London in the First World War, and therefore the first foreign military attack on London since medieval times. It is out by half a mile. The Zeppelin bombing raid began further north in Stoke Newington, when an incendiary landed on the roof of 16 Alkham Road. That house still stands, and a better-informed plaque was erected on the 100th anniversary in May 2015. The two plaques also disagree on the date. The earlier attempt reckons 30 May, while the updated plaque plumps for 31 May – presumably as the raid started close to midnight.

Other mistaken locations

Sometimes the plaque bestowers get the wrong building. This happened to the painter Richard Dadd. The Greater London Council originally placed his memorial on 16 Suffolk Street, near Leicester Square, in 1977. It was later discovered that Dadd lived at number 15, and the plaque was moved. The troubled commemoration is an unfortunate reflection of Dadd's life; the painter spent many years in psychiatric care, or what passed for it in Victorian England. A few blocks away is another possible misfit. The plaque to poet John Dryden on 43 Gerrard Street is, according to the authoritative Blue Plaque Guide, 'almost certainly ... on the wrong building and honours the house of Dryden's next-door neighbour'.

Perhaps the most famous example of plaque backtracking concerns Benjamin Franklin. Today, the scientist and statesman's house at 36 Craven Street, Westminster is well known, and serves as one of London's most treasured house museums. For 45 years, a plaque to Franklin adorned the front of a completely different house. The Society of Arts, the organization behind the 1869 commemoration, had fallen foul of street renumbering and picked the wrong building. The plaque was only removed during the demolition of the address in 1914, and put into storage. A few years back, the museum announced plans to display the brown memorial on the outside of the correct property. However, the building's Grade I listing made this unworkable, and today the plaque can be found down in the basement.

Motor mayhem

Another mistaken 'first' can be found in Harrow-on-the-Hill. Here, a prominently placed plaque remembers the 'first recorded motor accident in Great Britain involving the death of the driver'.* The crash occurred on Grove Hill on 25 February 1899. A party of military types was out on an experimental motoring run up and down Harrow Hill. They reached the top without incident, but quickly hit trouble on the downward journey. According to a local press report, 'While the car was going down Grove Hill at a high speed the front wheel collapsed, and the occupants were violently thrown out.' The driver, Edwin Root Sewell (31), died instantly. A passenger called Major Ritche died later from a fractured skull and a further four passengers received minor injuries.

A tragic early motoring accident, for sure – but not the first. That unenviable record goes to Henry Lindfield of Brighton. Almost exactly a year before the Harrow accident, Mr Lindfield lost control of his motor waggonette during a drive through Purley, near Croydon. His vehicle ran through a wire fence and hit a tree, fatally injuring the driver. No plaque marks the site.

---

*FOOTNOTE: The plaque is presented in large capital letters, facing oncoming traffic at driver's-eye height, right in the middle of a fork in the road – it's as though someone wanted to cause another accident by distracting passing motorists. This is surely the only plaque in the kingdom that is both wrong and dangerous.

Dickensian duncery

Until recently, a brown plaque on the southern end of London Bridge noted the presence of Nancy's Steps. This short flight, leading down to Southwark Cathedral, has a feel of olden days, for the steps are too narrow to have been created in modern times. According to the missing plaque, 'The steps were the scene of the murder of Nancy in Charles Dickens's novel *Oliver Twist*.' They are often referred to as 'Nancy's Steps' today, despite the absence of signage.

It is peculiar that such a notorious and violent scene could be misremembered, but the murder did not take place on the bridge or the steps. The scene occurs in Chapter 47. Bill Sikes believes that his prostitute lover Nancy has betrayed him. He dashes home with 'savage resolution' to find Nancy lying on their bed. It is in their shared room, not on the bridge, that he strikes her dead with a heavy club.

The confusion has at least two origins. First, a similar flight of steps is mentioned elsewhere in the novel. Nancy keeps a liaison on London Bridge, but fears for its exposed location. 'Not here,' she says, 'I am afraid to speak to you here. Come away – out of the public road – down the steps yonder!' And down they go. This is the place where Nancy is overheard while revealing information about Sikes's associates – an act that precipitates her murder in the next chapter – but it is not the scene of the murder itself. The second source of confusion is *Oliver!*, the 1968 musical. In this most popular of film adaptations, the murder takes place at the foot of a flight of steps leading up to the bridge, albeit ones that look very different to the Nancy's Steps we know today.

The erroneous plaque went missing a few years ago. It was screwed into the wall close to the bottom of the narrow stairs, where it became a source of obstruction, as people stopped to read its mistaken content. Nevertheless, the steps are worth seeing. Along with the neighbouring arch, they are among the surviving fragments of the previous incarnation of London Bridge, the nineteenth-century span sold to an American businessman in the 1960s.

Official typos

The City of Westminster seems to be a happy hunting ground for commemorative errors. We've already seen the Dadd, Dryden and Franklin mislocations. Just a short stroll away on Tavistock Street, one finds a Greater London Council blue plaque to 'Thomas de Quincy', which should read 'de Quincey'. Perhaps it's fitting that one of the nineteenth century's most noted drug users, and the author of *Confessions of an English Opium Eater*, should be lacking an 'e'. To pick on Westminster with one final example, author George Moore's home on Ebury Street received a blue plaque in 1936. It lasted less than a year before the *Spectator* pointed out that his birthdate was wrong – 1851 instead of 1852. It was soon corrected.

Even today, the authorities make a surprising number of errors. In 2015, the Borough of Hillingdon erected a sign misspelling its neighbouring authority as 'Hownslow' rather than 'Hounslow'. In the same year, the London Overground station of Theobalds Grove was signed as 'Theobolds Grove', while Walthamstow became 'Waltamstow'. Meanwhile, a nearby cycle path was decorated with signs to 'Walthamsow'. The prize for the dumbest mistake must, however, go to the Royal Parks. Its 2012 viewfinder plaque at the top of Primrose Hill mislabelled the elegant Caledonian clock tower as 'Holloway Prison'.

Deliberate typos

Not all typographical anomalies are accidental. The A–Z road atlas supposedly contains dozens of deliberate 'mistakes' – lanes that do not exist, for example, or misspelled street names, or false curves in roads. The deliberate fictions are known as 'trap streets', so named because they entrap any would-be plagiarist who copies the map without permission. While the layout of the streets themselves cannot be copyrighted, a particular artistic rendering can. Adding 'trap streets' allows the publisher to spot if somebody else has skipped all the hard surveying work and simply copied their own research, mistakes and all.

A peculiar example could once be found in Haggerston Park in east London. The park boasts a ski slope in older versions of the A–Z, but alas not in reality. That oddity is no longer printed, but other deliberate errors exist. I've had one or two pointed out to me, but my lips are sealed. Needless to say, map publishers do not comment on where their deliberate traps might lie. A number of examples can be found on the Internet, but most have since been expunged, presumably replaced by new trap streets elsewhere. If nothing else, trap streets give the publisher a ready-made excuse if someone spots a genuine error in their work.

Bankside oddness

Another famous fallacy can be found in Bankside. Look to the right of Shakespeare's Globe and you'll find a quaint row of old houses that are neither from Shakespeare's time nor our own. On the tallest, a whitewashed property, you'll spy a plaque to the memory of Sir Christopher Wren. The architect supposedly lived in the house during the construction of St Paul's Cathedral (i.e. the early eighteenth century). One can picture the great man gazing out of the upper-storey window, fondling his periwig while musing on his masterwork across the Thames. The lower part of the plaque goes even further back, asserting that: 'Catherine Infanta of Castille and Aragon' took shelter here in 1502, upon her first arrival in London.

That's quite a guest book. Unfortunately, it's all supposition. The house itself is barely old enough for Wren, let alone the Tudor queen-to-be. It was completed in 1710, coeval with St Paul's Cathedral. So, if Wren did use it, he can only have witnessed the very last lick of paint. According to historian Gillian Tyndall, an earlier Wren plaque could once be found in these parts, attached to the wall of another Bankside house. When that was demolished, the plaque shifted to a wall near Bankside power station (now Tate Modern). The plaque was then lost at some point, but its memory lived on. The current memorial is in yet another location and is a mid-twentieth-century pastiche.

The apologetic plaque

While most memorials commemorate individuals, groups or historic events, one central London plaque eats humble pie. In the north-west corner of Russell Square, where Thornhaugh Street decants into the School of Oriental and African Studies, an understated stone tablet makes the following grovel: 'The University of London hereby records its sincere apologies that the plans of this building were settled without due consultation with the Russell family and their trustees and therefore without their approval of its design.'

The offending building went up in 1988, and would eventually house the Brunei Gallery (which, incidentally, has a smashing little Japanese garden on the roof, if you ever care to visit). It's not an unattractive building, fitting in neatly with the Georgian terraces to the south and opposite. It even won a Civic Trust award for it tasteful lines. So who objected and why?

The Russell family, fronted by the Duke of Bedford, are the historic landowners of much of the area, with holdings that once stretched from what is now Euston Road to Covent Garden. Chunks of the Bedford estate were sold off in the first half of the twentieth century. The University of London, seeking to expand, lapped up several acres. As an educational establishment, it had the power of compulsory purchase, and the Russell family could not block it from buying up whatever land it required. The dynasty did, however, insist on a condition of sale. It wanted to have the right of approval over any new building planned at a sensitive viewpoint. The Brunei Gallery is one such site, overlooking Russell Square and its Georgian terraces. Although the family were shown early plans, the university got ahead of itself and commissioned the building without the Russell family's rubber stamp. To make amends, the university agreed to place the plaque on the side of the building in 1995, with a design and wording specified by the Russell family. It remains there today, probably the only plaque in the world to convey 'sincere apologies'. How very English.

And now for something completely different ...

The most entertaining 'wrong plaque' of them all can be found in the courtyard of Shakespeare's Globe. Here, the floor is covered with small nameplates giving the names of the many donors to the theatre. Among them is a certain 'Michael Pallin'. The misspelling is apparently intentional. The flagstone was bought by fellow Python John Cleese, who mischievously requested that his friend should be immortalized as 'Pallin' rather than 'Palin', the correct version. I've never had this one officially verified, but the Globe's own tour guides habitually repeat it.

Tourist-trap trivia

This final chapter is a miscellanea. Below, you'll find many a well-known 'fact' beloved of the popular press, trivia compilers and the lazier species of tour guide.

You're never more than six feet away from a rat

Unless you live in the sewers or happen to own a pet rat, this oft-repeated truism is self-evidently nonsense. Think about it. How regularly do you see rats in London? Personally, I spot one every three months or so, and usually when I'm in a woody environment.

Unlike mice, rats rarely infiltrate modern city buildings. It does happen, but it's rare. If you live or work above ground-floor level, then you're probably a long way from the nearest big rodent. The Food and Environment Research Agency estimates that just 3 per cent of UK households have rats living in the garden or surrounding land, while only 5 per cent of commercial premises are occupied by the animals. In cities like London, there is approximately one urban rat for every 5,000 sq. m (53,819 sq. ft). In other words, you are on average 50 m (164 ft) away from a rat.

Nobody knows where or when the 'six feet' myth started. It may well have been closer to the truth in centuries gone by, when dwellings were more porous, living conditions were more insanitary, and people spent much of their time outdoors. But the rat rate may be turning. A warmer climate and increased flood risks could see a rise in urban rat populations.

Savoy Court is the only place in London where you must drive on the right

The eye is easily drawn into Savoy Court, a small turning off the Strand. The art deco façade and entrance to the Savoy Hotel is one of London's minor landmarks. If you let your gaze linger, you might spot something decidedly odd about the court. Cars are instructed to enter via the right-hand lane, contrary to normal UK traffic regulations.

It is often claimed that Savoy Court is the only road in Britain where you must drive on the right. This is not quite true. Such a set-up is common at bus stations, for example. Bus doors are always on the left-hand side of a vehicle. Whenever the bus is serving an island bus shelter, it makes sense for it to approach from the right and loop anti-clockwise around the shelter, so that its doors always face into the island to allow boarding or disembarkation. Hammersmith bus station is a good example. Instructions to 'Drive on right' are clearly marked on the tarmac by the entrance.

'OK, but that's for buses only', you might retort. True, but there are many examples where cars and other private vehicles are required to drive on the right. The car park at Victoria station, for example, has a reversed layout. The set-up is potentially confusing for pedestrians crossing the entrance of the car park, who must remember to look for approaching vehicles in the non-intuitive direction. Even named roads can be right-handed. Petty France in the Square Mile has a cycle contraflow on the 'wrong' side of the road. Most impressive of all, if that's the right word, is the Tottenham Hale gyratory. Until recently, a short section known as 'the Hale' featured a reversed-direction dual carriageway. Vehicles were separated by a central partition, but they nevertheless proceeded in the 'wrong' direction. There are many other examples across the country.

But what's the Savoy's reason for its contrarian courtyard? The Savoy Theatre's entrance is on the right-hand side as you enter the road. Forcing vehicles to enter on the right allowed cabs to queue up to the doors of the theatre, without blocking the hotel entrance just beyond. Boring, but true.

Other inaccuracies persist with this legend. Look up the story online and you will find dozens of sites parroting a supposed Act of Parliament in 1902, which gave the hotel permission to reverse driving priority. No such act exists, and no record of a relevant debate is to be found in *Hansard*, the official record of the Houses of Parliament.

Neither I nor the Savoy's archivist have found any mention of official sanction. I suspect it was never given. The court was probably made right-handed in the early 1930s, when traffic enforcement was not as strict as it is today. My best guess is that the Savoy, being on private land, simply went ahead with its novel road scheme without any public debate or permission from the local authorities.

The set-up has not always worked harmoniously. Queues to turn right into the courtyard from the Strand caused major hold-ups in the 1960s. A policeman was stationed on the junction to help ease the flow. Right turns were eventually outlawed, although this has since been reversed.

Ever wondered why Brits drive on the left? The most common explanation, which appears to hold some truth, places the beginnings of the tradition on London Bridge. In 1722, Lord Mayor Gerard Conyers decreed that: 'All carts, coaches and other carriages coming out of Southwark into this City do keep all along the west side of the said bridge: and all carts and coaches going out of the City do keep along the east side of the said bridge.' In other words, 'Keep left'. The directive may have been arbitrary, or it may have been based on an earlier custom of driving on this side. Nobody really knows, but many just-so stories have been advanced. Some say that the Romans always marched on the left, and that the habit has remained with us through the centuries. Others point to a medieval origin. Sticking to the left of the road would place oncoming traffic to your right, and therefore in range of your sword arm (assuming you are right-handed). Your carriage could be defended from any approaching ne'er-do-wells. It's possible, though unproven.

A little-known Roman bathhouse can be found near the Strand

Just around the corner from the Savoy lurks a peculiar remnant of a bygone age, and another contender for our 'incorrect plaques' section. Head along Surrey Street towards the river, ignoring the intriguing former Strand Tube station. On the right, above an arch, you'll find a sign directing you to the 'National Trust Roman Bath'.

Through the arch, and to the right, you will indeed find what appears to be an ancient pool. It's usually locked away inside an old, white-painted brick building, but you can view it by peering through the window. A rectangular floor cavity does look for all the world like an old Roman bath, built with the narrow tiles characteristic of the period. And so it has been styled since at least Victorian times. Respected authority Walter Thornbury described it in 1878 as 'one of the oldest structures in London'. A faded nineteenth-century plaque inside the bathhouse attests to its Roman origins.

There is a serious flaw in the dating. The Roman city of Londinium was a good 800 m (half a mile) to the east. While Roman coins, coffins and sherds have been found around the Strand area, no significant building structures are known in these undefended parts outside the wall. Based on its depth below modern street level, most experts now agree that the bathhouse is from the seventeenth century. It may have been used as a cistern for fountains at nearby Somerset House, or else served as a mock-classical pool for former landowner the Earl of Arundel to lord it like a Roman emperor. Either way, the spring-fed pool was used as a bath for many years, and was open to the general public throughout the nineteenth century. Dickens has David Copperfield plunging into a bath on this site.

Today, you can visit the so-called Roman bath by appointment with Westminster Council, which keeps an eye on the place on behalf of the National Trust. It is also accessible on Open House weekend every September. Just don't expect to take a dip.

An old street lamp on Carting Lane is powered entirely by the fumes from sewers

The area around the Savoy, it seems, is littered with urban myths. Carting Lane runs just to the west of the hotel, sloping steeply down to the Thames. Part way along, you'll find a chunky old lamp post, which does indeed still burn gas.* Legend has it that the lamp, dubbed 'Iron Lily', runs entirely on methane given off by the Savoy's sewer system. In other words, this is the only lamp in London powered by the turds of posh people. It has led to a popular punchline among tour guides: Carting Lane is mockingly referred to as Farting Lane.

It's a great tale, so I'm pleased to report that it does rest on a whiff of truth. The lamp was one of several installed by inventor Joseph Webb in the 1890s. It was designed to burn off sewer gas, both to prevent the gradual build-up of explosive quantities, and to neutralize bad smells. Even with a full house of defecating lords, however, the Savoy's sewers would not produce enough methane to keep the lamp in constant luminosity. It was always powered by regular mains gas. The feculent fumes from below provided only a minor contribution.

Iron Lily got into an argument with a reversing lorry a few years ago, and was badly mangled. The lamp post we see today is a reconstruction, powered now, as always, by mains gas. Nevertheless, one should offer a respectful bottom parp whenever one passes this Thames-side curiosity.

---

*FOOTNOTE: Contrary to popular belief, London still retains a fair population of gas lamps. Around 1,300 still grace the streets, with another 200 on private property. They are maintained by a team of four engineers from British Gas.

Black cab drivers must carry a bale of hay everywhere they go

This little nugget falls into the category of 'ancient laws never repealed'. One can readily imagine a time when cabs were pulled by horses, and a bale of hay would have served as the equivalent of diesel in the modern motor. Most cabbies I've asked about the legend chuckle to themselves and tell me it's completely true. They're still required by law to drive around with a bale of hay in the boot. None of them do, of course.

The commandment seems to have no basis in law. The closest Westminster came to forcing bales of hay on cabbies comes in the London Hackney Carriage Act of 1831. Section 51 of this Act concerns itself with the many ways in which drivers might block the street – one of which involves horse feed. Drivers must not: 'feed the Horses of or belonging to any Hackney Carriage in any Street, Road or common Passage, save only with Corn out of a Bag, or with Hay which he shall hold or deliver with his Hands'.

The Act does not require the cabman to carry any food at all, stipulating only that feeding must be done from the hand and not block the carriageway with bales or troughs. The penalty for such a misdemeanor was 20 shillings. If a modern cab driver attempted to place a bale of hay in front of her vehicle, her 20 shillings would be safe. The legislation was quashed as part of the Statute Law (Repeals) Act of 1976.

London's equestrian statues conform to a hidden code

A popular urban myth in many countries holds that you can work out how someone died by the attitude of his or her horse in an equestrian statue. If one hoof is lifted, the rider sustained serious injuries in battle, possibly dying later. If two hooves are raised, he died in battle. All four hooves on the ground indicate that the rider was never injured in battle and died by other means.

London contains at least 15 equestrian statues of named individuals. These are summarized below in alphabetical order. A cross indicates that the statue does not satisfy the legend. A tick means that it does.

Albert, Prince Consort (Holborn). One hoof up. Victoria's husband was an intellectual, not a warrior, and never sustained a battle wound. ✖

Charles I (Charing Cross). One hoof up. He was never wounded in battle, as far as is known. ✖

Duke of Wellington (Hyde Park Corner). All hooves down. The Iron Duke sustained only minor injuries in his military campaigns, not worth commemorating in statue. ✔

Duke of Wellington (Royal Exchange). All hooves down. A second equestrian statue which agrees with the first. This statue is also peculiar in lacking stirrups. ✔

Edward VII (Waterloo Place). One hoof up. The monarch died in old age. Appropriately, his final words concerned a horse racing result. ✖

Ferdinand Foch (Victoria). All hooves down. The First World War French soldier lived long and prospered without serious injury. ✔

Garnet Wolseley, First Viscount Wolseley (Horse Guards Parade). All hooves down. This exceptionally decorated soldier and field marshal is mostly forgotten today, but served with distinction in many campaigns, including Crimea. He was badly injured on one occasion, but eventually died in old age. ✔

Earl Haig (Whitehall). One hoof up. The First World War commander evaded serious injury, despite presiding over the Western Front and its unimaginable carnage. He died of a heart attack in later life. ✘

George III (Pall Mall). One hoof up. He never fought a battle. ✘

George IV (Trafalgar Square). All hooves down. The fat old king never saw combat and died in bed after a painful, withering gastric illness. ✔

George, Duke of Cambridge (Whitehall). All hooves down. The last Duke of Cambridge (until 1904) before the current one assumed the title (Prince William) served in the military, but was never badly injured. ✔

Sir George Stuart White (Portland Place). Four hooves down. The soldier and VC winner got through many a scrape and lived to a decent age. ✔

Richard the Lionheart (Palace of Westminster). One hoof up. The unfortunate king died of gangrene two weeks after taking an arrow during a siege in France. ✔

Lord Roberts (Horse Guards Parade). Four hooves down. The Victorian soldier lived to a ripe old age, dying of pneumonia. ✔

William III (St James's Square). Two hooves up. He did not die in battle, but after falling from his horse, which supposedly stumbled on a molehill (represented in the statue). ✘

In conclusion, nine of the 15 equestrian statues match the code, showing that it is not a reliable system for reading the fate of any particular rider.

One final monument worth considering is the statue of Oliver Cromwell, leader of the country during our brief experiment with republicanism in the 1650s. His likeness stands outside the Palace of Westminster close to Richard the Lionheart. Old Ironsides does not sit on a horse, although there had been many calls for an equestrian statue before this horseless figure was unveiled in 1899. Nevertheless, Cromwell appears to anticipate a ride, judging from his impressive pair of spurs. It is often said that he wears the spurs upside down, perhaps as a deliberate symbol of overturning the system from a monarchy to a republic. However, it is not hard to find paintings from the period that show similarly booted figures.

There are no roads in the City of London

One of the great pieces of London trivia posits that the City of London contains not a single thoroughfare that carries the word 'Road' in its name. You'll find plenty of examples of 'Street', 'Hill', 'Alley' and 'Square', but never a 'Road'.

This was probably the case for much of London's history. Until modern times, a street (from the Latin *via strata*, meaning 'a laid-down way') was normally a paved thoroughfare within a town centre. A road, by contrast, usually led away from town (cf. the Uxbridge Road) or between nearby towns. The City of London has been densely settled for 1,000 years, so any roads such as City Road and Goswell Road begin outside its well-defined and ancient borders.

This was true up until 1994. In that year, boundary changes did away with centuries of tradition. The City expanded north to take in the Golden Lane Estate. In doing so, it absorbed Goswell Road, bringing a road within the boundaries of the City for the first time. I'm told that the change was not made in ignorance, and that some members of the Corporation council argued vociferously for a name change, to preserve the historic absence, but to no avail.

This overturned piece of trivia can still cling desperately to a life-preserving piece of pedantry. The boundary line runs along the middle of Goswell Road: the western half is in the Borough of Islington while the eastern half alone rests within the Square Mile. So it can still be said that there is not a *single* road in the City of London, merely a half road.

Ely Place is technically in Cambridgeshire and you can't be arrested there

There are certain 'hidden gems' that no trivia book about 'alternative London' ever omits. You may have heard of the wall of heroic sacrifice in Postman's Park, or the supposedly little-known Sir John Soane's Museum and its rooms of antique treasures. Add to that list the short cul-de-sac of Ely Place.

The side street lies immediately north-east of Holborn Circus. It has some form of special status, as is clear from the small lodge and barrier that guard its entrance. Those 'hidden gem' guidebooks will tell you that this is a frontier with Cambridgeshire; that the land beyond the barrier is owned by the bishops of Ely. This throws up any number of anomalies. The Metropolitan Police, for example, have no jurisdiction over the enclave and must apply for permission to enter – much to the delight of fleeing crooks. We are also told that a costumed beadle still presides over the gate and will call the hours throughout the night.

Like any good story, there is a kernel of historical truth here. The lands did indeed once belong to the bishops of Ely, and were administered from Cambridgeshire. Beadles maintained the peace, or broke it with their hourly cries. However, all this malarky died out many decades ago.

The beadles seem to have cleared off sometime around the end of the Second World War. A newspaper article from 1940 describes an encounter with one of their number. They still shouted out the time and the weather but, quipped the reporter, 'Due to wartime restrictions they may only impart the latter information after it is a fortnight old.'

The old canard about the police not being allowed access without permission is repeated in reports from the nineteenth and early twentieth centuries. If the restriction ever did exist,* it was not observed. Police were quick on the scene in 1925, for example, when £20,000-worth of jewels were stolen from a repository on the street. The ineffectual beadles heard nothing.

Today, the cul-de-sac is a quiet backwater, a private road cut off from the hurly-burly of Holborn and Farringdon. It still feels like an enclave. No uniformed beadle guards the barrier at the entrance, but a suited security guard is sometimes to be found in the gatehouse. It is no longer considered part of Cambridgeshire, if it ever was, but is supervised by the Commissioners of Ely Place, located at number 28. This property management company is the successor of a body set up by Act of Parliament in 1842, which provided 'commissioners for paving, lighting, watching, cleansing and improving Ely Place and Ely Mews, Holborn, in the County of Middlesex'. Most of these functions are now handled by Camden Council, within whose jurisdiction Ely Place has been since 1963.

Part of Cambridgeshire it is not. The street does hold three treasures worth seeking out, however. First is the ancient church of St Etheldreda, said to be the oldest Catholic church in the country. Towards the end of the street, a series of brick arches suggest a railway viaduct. It is merely a boundary wall, but it holds a certain mystique. Occasionally, a gate in the wall is left open, and the curious explorer can pass through into the equally enigmatic Bleeding Heart Yard. I like to think of this as London's gateway to Narnia. Finally, Ye Olde Mitre pub lurks down Ely Passage, next to St Etheldreda's Church. This is reckoned to be one of the oldest pubs in London, and is certainly among the most difficult to find.

---

*FOOTNOTE: And why would it? A police officer can make an arrest in any part of the United Kingdom, not just his or her own territory.

The motif on Westminster's lamp posts is a memorial to Coco Chanel

Next time you're walking through the City of Westminster, take a close look at the black lamp posts. Many contain a motif that looks like two horseshoes linked together, or two letter Cs back-to-back. Remind you of anything?

The design resembles the logo of fashion designer and perfumer Coco Chanel, which reflects her initials. Is this an early example of corporate sponsorship? The story is more romantic. Chanel enjoyed a ten-year affair with the second Duke of Westminster. Legend says that the duke appended her initials to his street furniture as an amorous gesture. 'My dear Coco,' he might have said, 'I'd like to be reminded of you every time I inspect my bollards.'

Sadly for romantics everywhere, the story is apocryphal. The 'CC' device merely stands for 'City Council', and it's usually accompanied by a fancy 'W' indicating 'Westminster'. The lamp posts were installed in the 1950s, long after Chanel had split with the duke. (The pair never married; the designer's cutting explanation: 'There have been several Duchesses of Westminster. There is only one Chanel.') A similar, but unconnected, motif can be found throughout the livery hall of the Clothworkers' Company in the Square Mile.

Perhaps it's time to start a new rumour: the 'CC' mark actually commemorates Charlie Chaplin, whose stellar career began on the West End stage.

Trafalgar Square contains the world's smallest police station

If the Edwardians had built a space capsule, it might have looked a little like the piece of street furniture at the south-east corner of Trafalgar Square. This bulbous granite rotunda narrows towards the top, and is surmounted by an oversized ornamental lamp. It is often described as Britain's (or the world's) smallest police station, and so it is marked on Google Maps.

It is no such thing – at least not today. If you peer through the windows, as I did 20 minutes before writing this paragraph, you'll find a dusty old storage space containing cleaning equipment. So anyone who tells you this *is* the world's smallest police station is wrong. There is a truncheon of truth in the story, however.

The pillar, like much of the square, was designed in by Sir Charles Barry, architect of the Houses of Parliament. It was installed in 1845, along with its near-twin in the south-west corner of the square. During the 1920s, redevelopment work called for the loss of a police box to the south. Rather than place a fresh structure to the side of the square, planners decided to hollow out one of the lamp pillars to create a subtle lookout point. It seems that the post was occasionally used by policemen to keep an eye on possible dissent in Trafalgar Square. It would be fanciful, however, to describe the structure as a police station.

Occasionally, you will hear a passing tour guide claim that the lamp on top comes from HMS *Victory*, the flagship of Horatio Nelson, whose stone effigy guards the square. If so, the *Victory* must have been mightily encumbered with ironmongery, for the square originally contained four of these giant lamps. Over a dozen similar structures can be found around the forecourt of Charing Cross station. In fact, they're the work of Messrs Stevens and Co. of south London and were built specifically for the square.

Marble Arch contains London's smallest police station

A marginally more convincing claimant for a police station is Marble Arch. This landmark at the western end of Oxford Street is not a solid mass of stone, but contains a series of rooms. The space has, on occasion, been used by the police force and park security personnel. In 1866, for example, a concealed contingent of police poured out of the arch to prevent a crowd of reformists from entering Hyde Park. According to one account, the constabulary seemed to 'rise from the ground' as over 100 officers emerged from the hiding place. The situation later descended into violence, not helped by the arrival of a party of mounted soldiers. The ensuing trouble was dubbed 'the Battle of Hyde Park' by the press.

The rooms maintained a police connection until 1968, when poet John Betjeman recorded a typically elegiac verse on top of the structure for the BBC's cameras. Before doing so, he's pictured inside the 'fully equipped police station', suitably accompanied by a uniformed officer. In truth, the 'station' looks abandoned and devoid of facilities. Indeed, there's scant evidence that the space was ever used as more than a mustering station, or lookout post. I can find no record of it serving as a place where members of the public might report crimes, or be locked in holding cells, as suggested by the term 'police station'. Accounts from 1900 speak of it merely as a useful base for the police during potential riots, and subservient to a much better-equipped police station elsewhere in the park. Let's call this one a half-truth.

Those citing Marble Arch as the smallest police station might be confusing it with Constitution Arch (sometimes called the Wellington Arch) at Hyde Park

Corner. This has a well-chronicled history of police use. According to a press report in 1922, around 16 'bachelor constables' were living inside this 'queer station'. The policemen specialized in traffic control and apparently lived in relative luxury. 'There is even a bathroom', marvelled the article.

Another myth surrounding Marble Arch, and repeated in the *London Encyclopedia*, is that only members of the royal family and members of the King's Troop Royal Horse Artillery may pass through it. The gates have stood open for as long as I can remember, and thousands of tourists pass through each day. They can't all be blue of blood or plain-clothes troopers.

Jeremy Bentham, the founder of University College London, still presides over council meetings, despite having died in 1832

Bentham was one of the great thinkers of his age, commenting on everything from prison reform to matters sexual. He's often cited as one of the founders of University College London. In truth, he played no role in its creation. The association has no doubt arisen from his many connections to the university today. A striking mural of Bentham studying the college plans can be found in the dome above the library – pure fiction, apparently. A nearby student pub is named after him. Most gloriously, his padded remains are still on show to anyone who cares to take a look.

In his will, Bentham left very specific instruction on the preservation of his body. His skeleton was to be swaddled in hay, dressed in his everyday clothes and put on show within the college. His head was to be embalmed and placed on top of his skeleton. Alas, the treated bonce had something of the zombie about it, and a wax replica was attached instead. The auto-icon, as this macabre assemblage is known, can be visited to this day. Simply walk into the main

UCL campus building, turn right into the south cloisters, and there sits the philosopher, staring out of his box.

It's often said that the Bentham auto-icon is wheeled into college council meetings with other senior staff. He is recorded in the minutes as 'present, but not voting'. It sounds like just the sort of eccentric British tradition that might have been maintained. Bentham, however, enjoys a contemplative retirement. His preserved form has only twice been wheeled into such a gathering – first, on the college's 150th anniversary in 1976; and again on the retirement of long-time provost Malcolm Grant in 2013. True to reputation, Bentham did not vote.

The Bentham head has also been the subject of myth-making. Until recent decades, the philosopher's mutilated noggin was displayed at the auto-icon's feet (the wax replacement on his shoulders). Legend says that the shrivelled member was stolen by rival students from King's College, and used in a game of football. I've had it confirmed from Bentham scholars that the head was indeed pilfered, in 1975. It was soon returned upon payment of a £10 ransom to charity. Fortunately, there is no evidence it was ever employed in a game of keepy-uppy. It would be too fragile to survive such a pummelling. The recovered head now resides under lock and key elsewhere in the college.

London tour guides are full of rubbish

And finally ... it might seem like I've set out to besmirch and traduce London's tour guides with this book. Nothing could be further from my intentions. I have the upmost respect for the profession and, to borrow a famous defence, many of my best friends are tour guides. As with any activity, there are good tour guides, bad tour guides and middle-of-the-road tour guides (actually, that final set succumb pretty quickly to insurance claims).

Nor do all tour guides cater only for tourists. A growing number put on regular walks for the curious Londoner or adventurous visitor who wants to explore parts of the city that most people miss. Over the years, I've been taken through the industrial estates of Dagenham Dock, into a branch of Iceland on Deptford High Street, round every single street in Soho, and offered a cup of tea in an East End boxing gym. One guide (Dave Brown of the Footprints of London group) even devised a walking tour of South Hampstead, in response to my declaration of it being London's most boring suburb. He showed me the error of my beliefs.

All of which is to affirm that I owe a great debt to London's tour guides, many of whom ply their trade as a labour of love as much as for the limited income it provides. I would encourage you to seek out the more innovative and knowledgeable of their number.

Of course, there are bad tour guides, too. Some lack passion for their subject or are simply jaded. Others have neglected their research and are happy to regurgitate the same old London 'facts'. Having read this volume, I hope that you are now suitably girded to resist such yarns.

Let's start a new wave of false facts

Having disproved many of the city's myths and legends, we need to find something to replace them:

- Jermyn Street in St James's is a contraction of 'Jeremy Corbyn Street'. The controversial politician was born at number 87.

- Greenwich Park is entirely devoid of starlings, and nobody knows why.

- London contains only one statue to Charles Dickens, but you wouldn't know it. A bronze representation of the novelist was erected during his own lifetime in Leicester Square. Dickens objected to the commemoration, so the likeness of Shakespeare was cast around it. Were you to crack open the Bard, you would still find Dickens imprisoned inside.

- One of the ravens at the Tower of London is actually albino. To maintain appearances, the Ravenmaster coats the bird in a special formulation of tar every fortnight. Look out for the bird with the pink eyes.

- London is technically still at war with Lincolnshire, owing to a special clause in Civil War legislature that was never fully repealed. The Tattershall Castle floating pub is named after a fortress in Lincolnshire – it set up moorings on the Thames in the 1980s as a subtle act of hostility.

- The bearskin hats worn by royal guards are made from real bearskin. To attain the privileged post, a soldier must kill and skin his own bear, whose pelt is then worked into the distinctive headgear.

- The Queen does not own her corgis. They are rented from Battersea Dogs' and Cats' Home.

- Tower Bridge has a hidden setting that allows the road bascules to slope down into the Thames. The feature provides landing ramps for ferries whenever the bridge is closed for repair.

- The statue of Eros actually depicts Prince Vultan, Brian Blessed's character in *Flash Gordon* (1980). The film received its premiere at the nearby Odeon cinema.

- To achieve its graceful curves, the Gherkin skyscraper is clad in futuristic hybrid glass. The advanced material is repellent to water, so window cleaners must use vinegar to wipe the surface.

- The Waterloo and City Tube line reuses an old escape tunnel dug by Dick Turpin in the 18th century.

- Just as black cab drivers must learn every street name in the capital to complete 'The Knowledge', London's tour guides must drink in every single pub before they're considered sufficiently qualified.

- The Thames was constructed in the 16th century to bring fresh water to the centre of London.

- The phrase 'sick as a parrot' was coined in London, inspired by Jimi Hendrix's beloved parakeet 'Little Wing Joe'. The bird's fondness for cannabis often left it comatose at the bottom of its cage. Monty Python's 'dead parrot sketch' was also a tribute to Joe.

Acknowledgements

With kind thanks to the numerous people who've helped track down answers or suggested London myths. In alphabetical order, they are: Sarah Bell, Peter Berthoud, Dave Brown, David Fathers, Marc Haynes, Sue Hillman, Anthony M. R. Lewis, Mark Mason, Ewan Munro, Richenda Walford, David Whittaker and Sarah Wise. Thanks also to Susan Scott, archivist of the Savoy Hotel, for a detailed response to my enquiries about the hotel. As ever, Guildhall Library must be toasted for its exceptional stores of London books and reference material. Finally, a big, big thank you to my wife Heather for turning her critical eye to an early draft of the manuscript, and for so much more besides.

I am happy to be contacted on i.am.mattbrown@gmail.com or Twitter @mattfromlondon.

Bibliography

Many sources were used in the research for this book, including countless newspaper articles and much archive material. Rather than list the whole damn lot, I've included a selection of the more helpful resources below, including books and websites namechecked in the text. For more detailed information on a particular point, please contact me on: i.am.mattbrown@gmail.com.

Books

Bolton, Tom. Vanished City: London's Lost Neighbourhoods. Strange Attractor, 2014.

Elborough, Travis. London Bridge in America: The Tall Story of a Transatlantic Crossing. Vintage, 2014.

Hanson, Neil. The Dreadful Judgment. Corgi, 2002.

Jones, Nigel. Tower. Windmill Books, 2012.

Martin, Andrew. Underground, Overground: A Passenger's History of the Tube. Profile Books, 2013.

Roud, Steve. London Lore. Arrow, 2010.

Sax, Bora. City of Ravens. The Overlook Press, 2012.

Weinreb, Ben, Christopher Hibbert, Julia Keay and John Keay. The London Encyclopedia, 3rd Edition. Macmillan, 2010.

Web resources

British Newspaper Archive: www.britishnewspaperarchive.co.uk; Diamond Geezer blog: http://diamondgeezer.blogspot.co.uk/; Ian Visits blog: http://www.ianvisits.co.uk/blog/; Londonist: londonist.com; Times Digital Archive: gale.cengage.co.uk/times.aspx/; Trove: trove.nla.gov.au/

The poem 'Always Touch In …' is by the author, but originally appeared on londonist. com. It is reproduced with permission.

Index